Observation Guide

for

Child Development in Action II

Laura E. Berk
Illinois State University

Allyn and Bacon
Boston London Toronto Sydney Tokyo Singapore

CONTENTS

PERSONALITY AND SOCIAL DEVELOPMENT CHAPTERS 10–13

Chapter 10 Emotional Development   67

Chapter 11 Self and Social Understanding   77

Chapter 12 Moral Development   87

Chapter 13 Development of Sex-Related Differences and Gender Roles   95

CONTEXTS FOR DEVELOPMENT CHAPTERS 14–15

Chapter 14 The Family   103

Chapter 15 Peers, Media, and Schooling 111

ANSWERS TO GETTING READY   117

SUGGESTIONS FOR OBSERVING AND INTERVIEWING YOUNG CHILDREN 120

ACKNOWLEDGMENTS

I am indebted to many people for the opportunity to convey the beauty, wonderment, and complexity of child development through this Observation Program and Guide, designed to accompany the fifth edition of my text, *Child Development*.

The staff of Instructional Technology, Television Production, at Illinois State University were my collaborators for over six months as we filmed, wrote script, edited footage, and assembled hundreds of segments into an integrated program. When I approached Jeffrey Payne, Writer/Producer, about taking on this project, to my good fortune he willingly agreed. Each moment of the film bears the mark of his artistry, craftsmanship, and sensitivity to our young participants. Under Jeff's direction, Steve Koch, Mitch Risinger, Rob Sutter, Tom Schmidt, Danny Sepesy, and Mark Vollstedt faithfully participated in over a hundred hours of filming and several weeks of editing, bringing their aesthetic and technical expertise to bear on all aspects of the program.

Many children, parents, and teachers are responsible for the diversity of settings, concepts, and developmental milestones depicted in the Observation Program. Marsha Riss, Vice Principal, devoted several days to working with me and the Metcalf School staff to schedule film shoots, making our visit to the school efficient and pleasurable. Karen Stephens, Director of the Illinois State University Child Care Center, made it possible for us to illustrate high quality child care and numerous developmentally appropriate learning activities for preschool children. I am grateful, also, to University High School, Illinois State University, for making possible interviews with students and filming of math and history classes. I thank Goodwood Children's Centre, Kalaya Children's Centre, Swallowcliffe School, and Access Arts of suburban Adelaide, South Australia, for permitting us to represent their unique early childhood, multicultural, cooperative learning, and art education programs, which lend a special international dimension to this revision. Finally, because of the openness of several American and Australian families to sharing their experiences with us, the video now contains a much richer depiction of the diversity of family lifestyles, including new segments on the transition to parenthood, adolescent childbearing, divorce and paternal custody, and dual earner families.

Finally, *Child Development in Action* is an outgrowth of my many years of gratifying, productive work with Allyn and Bacon. Sean Wakely, editor of my texts for nearly four years, encouraged me to expand the observation experiences I provide in my own classes into an instructional tool that could reach students everywhere. I am especially appreciative of his support and encouragement through the first edition and the planning stage of the revised edition. Carolyn Merrill, Executive Editor, has effected a smooth and gracious transition to a new editorial sponsorship and offered much wise counsel in the final filming and production stages. My appreciation, also, to Sue Gleason, Senior Developmental Editor, for many helpful suggestions for the makeup of the Observation Program and accompanying Observation Guide.

Laura E. Berk

INTRODUCTION

Child Development in Action—the Observation Program that accompanies your textbook—contains hundreds of segments specially selected to illustrate the many theories, concepts, and milestones of development you are about to study. This Observation Guide is designed to help you use the Observation Program in conjunction with the text to deepen your understanding of child development and apply what you have learned to everyday life.

USING THE OBSERVATION PROGRAM AND GUIDE

The Observation Program has thirteen sections, each of which corresponds to a chapter of your textbook. To assist with cueing the videotape, assuming your tape counter is set at zero, the right-hand column below indicates the elapsed time in hours, minutes, and seconds at which each main section begins:

Chapter	Tape Log		Chapter	Tape Log
• Chapter 3	0:02:49		• Chapter 10	1:09:37
• Chapter 4	0:12:32		• Chapter 11	1:16:19
• Chapter 5	0:24:02		• Chapter 12	1:31:40
• Chapter 6	0:30:23		• Chapter 13	1:37:46
• Chapter 7	0:47:25		• Chapter 14	1:42:19
• Chapter 8	0:57:52		• Chapter 15	1:52:39
• Chapter 9	1:05:26			

After reading each chapter, watch the associated section of the Observation Program. Then answer the questions and carry out the activities in the Observation Guide. Each chapter-linked section of the Observation Guide contains a brief summary of the observation segments and three types of learning experiences:

• **Mastering Course Content** These questions will assist you in using the Observation Program to master essential concepts and make course content more memorable. Answer them diligently, and you should do better on examinations. If you have difficulty with a particular question, refer to the textbook pages associated with it to review.

• **Building Connections** These exercises will help you use the Observation Program to see the interconnectedness among all aspects of development. Although each observation segment highlights a specific topic, every facet of development is related to others; the child grows as an integrated whole. The "Building Connections" section encourages you to review observation segments and many parts of the text, keeping in mind linkages among physical, cognitive, emotional, and social development as well as diverse contexts that support all aspects of children's functioning.

• **Applying Your Knowledge: Learning Activities** These activities involve observations and interviews of children, parents, and teachers; discussion with your classmates; and individual reflection, using segments of the Observation Program as a starting point. On page 121, you will find some helpful suggestions for observing and interviewing young children.

Each section of the Observation Guide is conveniently designed with perforated pages so it can be turned in as a course assignment.

GETTING READY: REVIEW OF BASIC CONCEPTS AND THEORIES

To make the most of the Observation Program, it is vital that you master basic concepts of development and the introduction to contemporary theories in Chapter 1 of your textbook. After reading Chapter 1, test your knowledge by answering the questions in this section. *Child Development in Action* will revisit these concepts and theories as they reappear in later chapters of your textbook. Note that here, and throughout the Observation Guide, questions are page-referenced to chapter content so you can easily refer to the text should you need to review. Once you have completed this section, check your answers against the key at the end of this guide.

BASIC ISSUES

1. Match each theoretical approach with its description: (6–9)

____ Accepts diverse pathways of change

____ Views development as adding on more of the same types of skills

____ Regards development as following one, univeral course for all children

____ Views environment as the most important influence in development

____ Regards early experiences as establishing lifelong patterns of behavior

____ Views heredity as the most important influence in development

A. Theory that stresses contexts

B. Stage theory

C. Continuous theory

D. Theory that stresses stability

E. Theory that stresses nature

F. Theory that stresses nurture

2. Define the concept of *stage,* and cite an example of behavioral change that would fit this definition. (8)

_____

_____

3. A theory that emphasizes _____ regards providing children with experiences aimed at stimulating change as of little value. (9)

4. True or False: In taking a stand on each of the three basic issues of child development, most modern theories recognize the importance of both sides. (9)

Resilient Children

A From Research to Practice box in Chapter 1 describes current findings on *resiliency*—the ability to spring back from adversity. Several children in the Observation Program fit the definition of resilient children: (1) Kristin, a child with Down syndrome who underwent six surgeries to correct a heart defect during her first 3 years; (2) Cara, a child who experienced birth complications; (3) Jacob, a child born to teenage parents; (4) Emily, a child abandoned shortly after birth in the People's Republic of China and reared in an unstimulating orphanage until 18 months of age; Dylan and Jeremy, whose parents are divorced and whose father has custody; Jeremy has cerebral palsy.

5. Name and describe three factors that shield resilient children from adversity: (10)
A. _____
B. _____
C. _____

6. On the basis of findings on resiliency, cite two approaches to intervention that can help safeguard children's development. (10)
A. _____
B. _____

After you have observed Kristin, Cara, Jacob, Emily, Dylan, and Jeremy, be prepared to use this information to account for each child's capacity to overcome stressful life events.

CONTEMPORARY THEORIES

Contemporary theoretical perspectives illustrated in the Observation Program include: Piaget's cognitive-developmental theory; information processing; ethology; ecological systems theory; Vygotsky's sociocultural theory; and the dynamic systems perspective.

Piaget's Cognitive-Developmental Theory

7. Describe the view of children emphasized by Jean Piaget's *cognitive-developmental theory*. (21)

_____

8. Match each of Piaget's stages with the appropriate description: (20)

____ Thinking becomes abstract.   A. Preoperational
____ Acting on the world with eyes, ears, and   B. Concrete
        hands is the chief characteristic of this stage.   operational
____ Development of representation, including   C. Formal
        language and make-believe play, flourishes.   operational
____ Reasoning becomes logical and better organized   D. Sensorimotor

9. Describe three major contributions of Piaget's theory. (22)
A. _____
B. _____
C. _____

10. Cite two recent challenges to Piaget's theory. (22)

A. _____
B. _____

Information Processing

11. According to the *information-processing approach,* the human mind is best viewed as _____. (23)

12. Why do information-processing theorists use flowcharts to represent mental operations? (23)

_____
_____
_____

13. In what basic way are information processing and Piaget's theory alike? In what basic way are they different? (24)
A. _____
_____
B. _____
_____

14. Cite a major strength of the information-processing approach. (24)

_____

15. Describe two limitations of the information-processing approach. (24)
A. _____
B. _____

Ethology

16. What is the focus of *ethology?* _____
_____.
(24–25)

17. What is meant by *imprinting?* What important developmental concept did findings on imprinting lead to? (25)
A. _____
B. _____

18. What is meant by a *sensitive period, and* how does it differ from a *critical period?* (25)

_____
_____

19. Explain how John Bowlby's *ethological view of attachment* differs from the behaviorist *drive reduction explanation.* (25)

_____
_____
_____

Vygotsky's Sociocultural Theory

20. Describe Vygotsky's *sociocultural theory*. (26)

_____

_____

_____

21. True or False: Piaget and Vygotsky both viewed cognitive development as a socially mediated process. (26)

21. According to Vygotsky, children learn culturally valued skills through: (26)
  A. discovering how to perform them on their own.
  B. the guidance of expert partners.

23. True or False: Because cultures select tasks for children's learning, children in every culture develop strengths not present in others. (26)

Ecological Systems Theory

24. Summarize the view of child development in *ecological systems theory*. (27)

_____

_____

25. Match each environmental level of ecological systems theory with the appropriate description or example: (27–30)

____ Relationship between the child's   A. Exosystem
     home and school   B. Chronosystem
____ The influence of cultural values   C. Mesosystem
____ The parent's workplace   D. Macrosystem
____ The child's interaction with parents   E. Microsystem
____ Temporal changes in the child's
     environments

26. Why is the person–environment system ever changing? _____

_____

_____. (29)

New Directions: Development as a Dynamic System

27. A new wave of theorists has adopted a *dynamic systems perspective* on development. What is meant by development as a dynamic system? (30)

_____

_____

_____

28. Why have researchers been attracted to this new view? (30)

_____

_____

_____

CHAPTER 3

BIOLOGICAL FOUNDATIONS, PRENATAL DEVELOPMENT, AND BIRTH

PARTICIPANTS

• Adena and Cooper, new parents of Charlie, age 4 months.

• Steve and Tonya, in their twenties when 3 1/2-year-old Kristin, who has Down syndrome, was born; Nicole, their younger daughter, who is 11 months old.

• Bonnie, age 40, and Art, age 60, expectant parents; their daughter Cara, age 6 weeks.

SUMMARY

This section contains three parent interviews: (1) Adena and Cooper discuss the experience of childbirth and the transition to parenthood. Their son, Charlie, is 4 months old. (2) Steve and Tonya faced a tragedy rare among couples in their twenties. Their first child, Kristin, was born with Down syndrome. Tonya and Steve describe their reaction to Kristin's birth and factors that helped them adjust to caring for a baby with serious disabilities and health problems. (3) Art, age 60, and Bonnie, age 40, were considerably older than most expectant parents when they discovered that Bonnie was pregnant. A month before Cara is due, they discuss Bonnie's high-risk pregnancy and their efforts to prepare for parenthood. After Cara's arrival, they describe their daughter's adjustment following a difficult birth and the family's adaptation to life with a new baby.

```
TAPE LOG
To view this section, cue tape to: 00:02:49.
```

MASTERING COURSE CONTENT

Interview with Adena and Cooper

1. Cooper was present during Adena's labor and delivery. According to research, why is social support helpful during childbirth? (110)

_____

_____

2. Adena and Cooper comment that it's hard to tell what Charlie's temperament is like, since he seems to change from one day to the next. Can infant temperament be predicted from prenatal measures? Explain. (96)

_____

_____

3. Cite stresses experienced by Adena and Cooper during the first few months of caring for Charlie. Charlie was full-term and healthy at birth. What additional stresses are introduced into a couple's relationship when a baby is preterm? (113–114) _____
_____
_____

4. What do heritability estimates say about the contribution of genetic factors to personality? Are Adena and Cooper likely to influence Charlie's personality development? Describe research in Chapter 3 that supports your answer. (119–120, 122)
A. _____
_____
B. _____
_____
_____

5. True or False: Charlie is among over 90 percent of babies born in the United States who are perfectly normal. (118)

Interview with Steve and Tonya

6. Kristin was born with Down syndrome, the (most/least) common chromosomal abnormality. It occurs in 1 out of every ____ live births. (81)

7. Kristin has the most frequent form of Down syndrome: *trisomy 21*. Describe how she inherited it. (81)
_____
_____

8. In what ways are Kristin's physical features typical of Down syndrome? How about her health problems? (82)
A. _____
_____
B. _____
_____

9. Cite the risk of having a child with Down syndrome for mothers, like Tonya, who bear children in their mid-twenties. _____ How about mothers in their mid-thirties? _____ Mothers in their mid-forties? _____ (82)

10. Down syndrome (rises/declines) dramatically with maternal age. Cite two explanations for this trend. (82)
A. _____
_____
B. _____
_____

11. True or False: The father's gametes are sometimes responsible for a child with Down syndrome. (82)

12. True or False: Down syndrome and other chromosomal abnormalities are related to advanced paternal age. (82)

13. The concept of *range of reaction* illustrates how heredity and environment work together to affect development. How has Down syndrome affected Kristin's range of reaction to environmental influences? (121)

_____

_____

14. Using the recently expanded notion of *canalization,* explain why it was important to treat Kristin's health problems and provide her with an enriched environment at the earliest possible age. (121–122)

_____

_____

Interview with Art and Bonnie

15. Bonnie describes heavy use of medical technology in monitoring Cara's prenatal development. She had an *amniocentesis.* What is this procedure? In view of Bonnie's age, why did her doctor recommend it? (83, 86)

A. _____

B. _____

16. Frequent *ultrasounds* (or, as Bonnie terms them, *sonograms)* were taken during Bonnie's pregnancy. What did these pictures reveal about Cara's development to Bonnie's doctor? (86) _____

_____

17. Bonnie explains that, like many career women, she put off the decision to have children, waiting for the perfect moment. First births to women in their thirties and forties have (increased/decreased) in recent years. (105–106)

18. Bonnie had some health problems that led to extensive medical monitoring during pregnancy and a complicated birth. When women without serious health difficulties are considered, prenatal problems (are/are not) more common for those in their forties than those in their twenties. (105)

19. Art and Bonnie attended Lamaze classes in hopes of experiencing natural childbirth. Cite the components of a typical natural childbirth program. (109)

A. _____
B. _____
C. _____

20. Although Bonnie's pregnancy was high risk and the birth was difficult, Cara is doing well. For at-risk infants like Cara, what is the best predictor of how well they are likely to develop in later years? (116)

_____

_____

9

BUILDING CONNECTIONS

1. Is the day-to-day instability of 4-month-old Charlie's temperament, reported by Adena and Cooper, consistent with research? Explain. (416)

_____
_____
_____
_____

2. What nutritional benefits does breast-feeding offer Charlie? What did Adena find surprising and somewhat stressful about breast-feeding? (193)

A. _____

B. _____

3. Although marital satisfaction often declines after the birth of a baby, Adena and Cooper's relationship remains strong and positive. Cite at least one factor that probably eased the transition to parenthood for Adena and Cooper. (561)

_____
_____
_____
_____

4. According to ecological systems theory (see Chapter 1, pages 27–30), children's environments are not static, but ever-changing. How did the arrival of Kristin's younger sister Nicole change Kristin's social environment in ways important for her development?

_____
_____
_____
_____
_____

5. Steve and Tonya comment that Kristin's physical problems at birth meant they had to learn to take care of her. How might illness and slow development influence the caregiving a child receives? What factors—within the family and the surrounding environment—probably assisted Steve and Tonya in providing Kristin the affection and stimulation she needed to develop at her best?

_____
_____
_____
_____
_____

6. Tonya notes that finding child care for Kristin was very difficult. Why is high-quality child care important not just for Kristin, but for her parents' adjustment and capacity to rear a child with disabilities? (See Chapter 10, page 434; Chapter 14, page 585–586.)

_____
_____
_____

Building Connections (continued)

7. Frequent ultrasounds enabled Art and Bonnie to see and interact with Cara before birth. Do you think ultrasound technology can affect parents' relationship with their baby? In what way?

_____
_____
_____
_____

APPLYING YOUR KNOWLEDGE:
LEARNING ACTIVITIES

1. Ask a young couple who have recently become parents about satisfactions and worries that accompany new parenthood. What factors are likely to make parenting easier? What factors might make it more difficult?

_____
_____
_____
_____
_____
_____
_____
_____
_____
_____
_____
_____
_____
_____
_____
_____
_____
_____
_____

2. Tonya comments that "she was not prepared at all" and "was very devastated" to learn that her newborn daughter had Down syndrome. Using ecological systems theory (Chapter 1, pages 27–30), design a hospital intervention program to help new parents accept the birth of a baby like Kristin. Keep in mind the importance of bidirectional influences between parent and child, social support, and connections between microsystems (such as home and hospital).

_____
_____
_____
_____
_____
_____
_____
_____
_____
_____
_____
_____
_____
_____
_____
_____
_____
_____

CHAPTER 4

INFANCY: EARLY LEARNING, MOTOR SKILLS, AND PERCEPTUAL CAPACITIES

PARTICIPANTS

Child	Age	To identify on video, look for...
Anna Marie	2 weeks	White, long-sleeved shirt and diaper, white socks
Cara	6 weeks	White, short-sleeved suit, bare legs and feet; later, pink sleep suit
Mac	3 months	Red shirt, blue overalls
Alex	5 months	Green playsuit
Hannah	7 months	Pink bow on head, multicolored playsuit with pink top
Randy	8 months	Yellow shirt, white jumpsuit
Nicole	11 months	White bow in hair, pink and white playsuit
Bailey	12 months	Red shirt, plaid overalls
Braxton	15 months	White shirt, black pants
Katherine	18 months	Blue shirt, blue striped overalls
Ben	21 months	White print shirt, tan pants
Zachary	23 months	Green, black, and white striped shirt
Kristin	3 1/2 years	White bow in hair, plaid playsuit

SUMMARY

This section begins with newborn capacities—reflexes that help ensure the baby will survive and receive care and attention from adults. Early learning—classical and operant conditioning, habituation and dishabituation, and newborn imitation—is also illustrated. Next, the Observation Program traces the attainment of a wide variety of motor skills during the first 2 years, pointing out factors that influence these milestones, individual differences, and implications for other aspects of development. This section concludes with examples of infant perceptual capacities and their intimate relationship to motor development.

> ## TAPE LOG
> To view this section, cue tape to: 00:12:32.

MASTERING COURSE CONTENT

Newborn Reflexes

1. Anna Marie, Cara, Mac, and Alex illustrate a variety of newborn reflexes. After watching the demonstrations, briefly describe the adaptive function of each: (128–130)

rooting _____
sucking _____
eye blink _____
withdrawal _____
Babinski _____
Moro _____
Palmar grasp _____
tonic neck _____
crawling _____
stepping _____
escape _____

2. Your textbook reviews only some of the newborn's reflexive capacities. Which of the reflexes listed above are *not* included in your text? (129)

_____   _____   _____

3. Select two newborn reflexes, and explain how each evokes care and attention from adults. (128–129)
A. _____
B. _____

4. Why did Professor Berk decide to illustrate reflexive capacities with babies no older than age 5 months? (129)

_____
_____

Learning Capacities

5. Tammy demonstrates *classical conditioning* of 2-week-old Anna Marie during feeding. Identify each of the components of classical conditioning in this example. (138–139)
unconditioned stimulus (UCS): _____
unconditioned response (UCR): _____
conditioned stimulus (CS): _____
conditioned response (CR): _____

6. Anna Marie's sucking can easily be classically conditioned. Other responses, such as fear, are more difficult to classically condition in young babies. Explain why. (139)

_____
_____

7. Professor Berk and Mac illustrate *operant conditioning*. What stimulus serves as

a reinforcer for Mac, increasing the probability that he will smile again? _____ What stimulus serves as a reinforcer for Professor Berk, increasing the probability that she will smile again? _____ (138–138)

8. Cara habituates to the green ring and then dishabituates to the yellow ring. These responses indicate that Cara (can/cannot) remember the green ring and (can/cannot) distinguish the green from yellow ring perceptually. (141–142)

9. On the basis of research presented in your text, is Anna Marie's imitation of Professor Berk's mouth opening an automatic response to stimulation or a flexible, voluntary capacity? Explain why. (142–143) _____
_____
_____

Motor Development

10. What theory described in the text views each motor attainment as a joint product of central nervous system maturation, movement possibilities of the body, environmental supports, and desire to explore and gain control over the surrounding world? _____ (163)

11. Using the example of 5-month-old Alex, who jumps with support from his father and struggles to crawl toward a rattle, explain why modern researchers argue that motor development cannot be a genetically prewired process. (146)
_____
_____

12. Look closely at 7-month-old Hannah. Cite an example of how gross motor development supports improvement in fine motor skills. (149)
_____
_____

13. Explain how motor capacities of 21-month-old Ben, who plays ball with Professor Berk, foster cognitive and social development. (144)
_____
_____
_____
_____
_____

14. Anna Marie, Cara, Alex, Randy, and Nicole illustrate the development of voluntary reaching. List their accomplishments, and explain how they conform to the *proximodistal trend* of motor development? (145)
_____
_____
_____
_____
_____
_____

15. Kristin's early experiences slowed her rate of motor development and also changed its form. In what way were her experiences similar to those of the Iranian babies observed by Wayne Dennis? (147)

_____
_____
_____
_____

Perceptual Capacities

16. How do Anna Marie, Cara, Hanna, and Nicole illustrate research findings on infants' sound perception? (153–154)
A. Responsiveness to the human voice (Anna Marie): _____

_____

B. Responsiveness to sound patterns (Cara, Hanna, and Nicole): _____

_____
_____
_____

17. Alex, Hannah, Bailey, and Braxton's responses to depth-at-an-edge (are/are not) consistent with research on the relationship of independent movement to depth perception. Summarize those findings. (158–159)

_____
_____
_____
_____

18. According to _differentiation theory,_ perception is guided by discovery of _affordances._ What does this mean? How do motor skills affect Alex, Hannah, Bailey, and Braxton's different views of the action possibilities a drop-off _affords?_ (166–167)
A. _____

_____
B. _____

_____
_____
_____

BUILDING CONNECTIONS

1. As we will see in Chapter 10, a secure attachment bond is built through adult sensitivity and responsiveness to infant signals. According to ethological theory (Chapter 1, page 25), behaviors of babies encourage parents to approach, care for, and interact with them. Explain how newborn reflexes and other infant motor capacities of the first year play an important role in the development of attachment, citing examples.

_____
_____
_____
_____
_____
_____
_____
_____
_____
_____
_____
_____
_____

2. Because of her early experiences, Kristin scoots instead of crawls. Observe Kristin's scooting again. How is this manner of moving about likely to affect exploration? Do you think Kristin's scooting contributed to the fact that at age 3, she has not yet begun to walk on her own? Explain why.

_____
_____
_____
_____
_____
_____
_____
_____
_____
_____
_____
_____

3. Cara's mother Bonnie is a professional singer who practiced and performed often during her pregnancy. Describe research indicating that Cara's special responsiveness to her mother's singing may have been learned before birth. (Chapter 3, page 94)

_____
_____
_____
_____
_____
_____
_____
_____
_____

Building Connections (continued)

4. As the text notes, researchers believe that crawling is so important in structuring babies' experience of the world that it may promote a new level of brain organization (see page 159). Look ahead to Chapters 6 and 10, and note cognitive and emotional milestones that emerge around the same time as crawling, and record them below.

Cognitive (Chapter 6, page 225) _____

_____
_____
_____
_____

Emotional (Chapter 10, page 403, 405, 408)

_____

_____
_____
_____

APPLYING YOUR KNOWLEDGE:
LEARNING ACTIVITIES

1. Parental beliefs about infant development vary from culture to culture. Some parents think that training children in motor skills is essential. Others believe that no special training or practice is necessary. Ask two or three parents, preferably of different ethnic backgrounds, about how they handle the motor development of their babies. How important does each parent think it is to encourage crawling, standing, walking, and other motor milestones? To what extent do you think culture plays a role in their responses?

_____
_____
_____
_____
_____
_____
_____
_____
_____
_____
_____
_____
_____
_____
_____
_____
_____
_____
_____

2. Perception and action are intimately related. Observe an infant or toddler at play for 15 minutes and record the child's gross and fine motor skills. Explain how the child's experiences in moving about independently and manipulating objects contribute to: (a) pattern perception; (b) depth perception; (c) object perception; and (d) intermodal perception.

_____
_____
_____
_____
_____
_____
_____
_____
_____
_____
_____
_____
_____
_____
_____

CHAPTER 5

PHYSICAL GROWTH

PARTICIPANTS

Child	Age	To identify on video, look for ...
Anna Marie	2 weeks	White long-sleeved shirt and diaper, white socks
Cara	6 weeks	White, short-sleeved suit, bare legs and feet; later, pink sleep suit
Alex	5 months	Green playsuit
Katherine	18 months	Blue shirt, blue striped overalls

• Children and teachers at Thomas Metcalf Laboratory School and the Child Care Center, Illinois State University
• Joel, age 18, Rhiannon, age 18, and Jacob, their 1-year-old son
• Ray and Laurie, Joel's parents

SUMMARY

In this section, overall trends in physical growth are described, including the cephalo-caudal trend; changes in body size, proportions, and composition; and implications for motor accomplishments in childhood and adolescence. Excerpts from the children's circus at Metcalf School illustrate sex-related differences in physical growth at puberty.

When adolescents become sexually active without using contraception, the consequences can be profound, as Rhiannon and Joel's story reveals. After dating Joel for a year, Rhiannon discovered that she was pregnant. Joel and Rhiannon share their reactions to the pregnancy and describe how the arrival of Jacob, their son, has changed their lives. Ray and Laurie relate their concerns about the effect of adolescent parenthood on their son's future.

> ## TAPE LOG
> To view this section, cue tape to: 00:24:02.

MASTERING COURSE CONTENT

The Course of Physical Growth

Compare the body size, proportions, and body fat of Anna Marie, Cara, and Alex. Then answer the following questions:

1. The narrator notes, "At first the head and chest have a growth advantage, but the trunk and legs gradually pick up speed." What growth trend is being described? (176) _____

2. Five-month-old Alex has accumulated considerably more body fat than 2-week-old Anna Marie and 6-week-old Cara. What is taking place in brain growth over the first 2 years that is supported by the high fat content of human milk? (193)

_____

3. Katherine, at 18 months, is losing her babyish appearance. What is happening to Katherine's growth that makes her look more like a little girl than a baby? (177)

_____
_____

4. Alex's father commented off-camera that Alex is a "good eater." Twenty-one-month old Ben's appetite, in contrast, has lessened, and he is becoming pickier about the foods he eats. How is this change in quantity of food eaten related to body growth? Explain why young children's wariness of new foods may be adaptive? (194)

A. _____
B. _____
_____
_____

Puberty: The Physical Transition to Adulthood

5. At puberty, large sex-related differences in body size, proportions, and composition appear. After observing the adolescents in the children's circus, describe these physical differences. (174–177)

_____
_____
_____
_____
_____
_____
_____
_____

6. What implications do sex-related differences in physical growth have for the development of motor skills? (180–181).

_____
_____
_____
_____

7. What does the children's circus reveal about the extent to which athletic accomplishment—including strength and speed (at which boys usually excel) and balance and dexterity (at which girls usually excel)—can be encouraged in children of both sexes? (180–181)

_____
_____
_____
_____

8. Timing of pubertal maturation has implications for adolescents' self-perceptions

and social adjustment. Describe these effects, noting sex-related differences. (206–207)

_____
_____
_____

9. Provide two explanations for the maturational timing effects. (207)
A. _____
_____
B. _____
_____

10. Metcalf School is a K–8 school. How are early maturing girls at Metcalf likely to fare in adjustment compared with girls in K–6 schools? Why? (207)

_____
_____
_____
_____

Adolescent Pregnancy and Parenthood

11. Rhiannon and Joel's story is not unique. Each year, more than a million American teenagers become pregnant. The United States has the highest rate of adolescent pregnancy and parenthood in the Western industrialized world. What three factors make American teenagers so vulnerable to early pregnancy? (214)
A. _____
B. _____
C. _____

12. Joel and Rhiannon decided not to marry. Nevertheless, both have taken on the responsibilities of parenthood. What is unique about Joel's response to parenthood? (217)
A. _____
_____
B. _____
_____

13. The narrator states that adolescent parenthood can have profound consequences for three generations. Describe its potential consequences for (a) Joel and Rhiannon; (b) Jacob; and (c) Ray and Laurie. (215)
A. _____
_____
B. _____
_____
C. _____
_____
_____

BUILDING CONNECTIONS

1. Although 5-month-old Alex has accumulated body fat, his stepping reflex is plainly evident. Why does adding body fat usually lead the stepping reflex to disappear by age 2 months? Alex enjoys being upright and jumping. Describe research indicating that these experiences might have contributed to his retention of the stepping response. (Chapter 4, page 130)

A. _____
_____
_____
_____

B. _____
_____
_____
_____
_____

2. Adolescents' adultlike appearance and sexual maturity trigger increased psychological distancing between parents and children. Explain this link between the physical and emotional domains of development. (Chapter 5, page 206)

_____
_____
_____
_____
_____
_____
_____
_____
_____
_____
_____
_____

3. Early adolescence is a time of increased gender stereotyping of interests, attitudes, and behavior. How might the arrival of puberty contribute to this trend? (Chapter 13, page 541)

_____
_____
_____
_____
_____
_____
_____
_____
_____
_____
_____
_____

Building Connections (continued)

4. Is Rhiannon more likely than other girls her age to remain a never-married single parent? (Chapter 5, page 215.) How well do children of never-married single parents fare in development compared with children in two-parent families? What factors account for the difference? (Chapter 14, page 577.)

_____
_____
_____
_____
_____
_____
_____
_____
_____
_____
_____
_____

APPLYING YOUR KNOWLEDGE: LEARNING ACTIVITIES

1. School-age children clearly profit from instruction in motor skills, as the physical education class and circus at Metcalf School reveal. But there is no evidence that preschoolers exposed to formal lessons are ahead in motor development. Instead, the physical environment in which informal play takes place makes a difference. Visit several public playgrounds in your community, and describe the play spaces and equipment available. Then evaluate the extent to which these environments are likely to stimulate young children's running, climbing, jumping, and throwing. What improvements would you make?

_____
_____
_____
_____
_____
_____
_____
_____
_____
_____
_____
_____
_____
_____
_____
_____

2. The text indicates that *secular trends in physical growth*—changes in body size and rate for growth from one generation to the next—have taken place in industrialized nations (see page 184). Record for yourself, your same-sex parent, and a same-sex grandparent adult height and the approximate age at which it was attained. (If you cannot obtain this information from your own family members, ask a friend to provide it on his or her family.) To what extent are your findings consistent with the existence of a secular trend? What factors probably account for secular trends in physical growth?

_____
_____
_____
_____
_____
_____
_____
_____
_____
_____
_____
_____
_____
_____

Applying Your Knowledge: Learning Activities (continued)

3. Do you know personally, or do any of your friends know personally, an adolescent parent? Did he or she graduate from high school? Enroll in college? How well are the parent and child faring in development now? What factors do you suspect contributed to favorable or unfavorable outcomes, and how well do those factors match research on the consequences of adolescent parenthood, reported in the text? (Chapter 5, pages 214–216.)

_____
_____
_____
_____
_____
_____
_____
_____
_____
_____
_____
_____
_____
_____
_____
_____
_____
_____
_____
_____
_____
_____

CHAPTER 6

COGNITIVE DEVELOPMENT: PIAGETIAN AND VYGOTSKIAN PERSPECTIVES

PARTICIPANTS

Child	Age	To identify on video, look for . . .
Alex	5 months	Green playsuit
Randy	8 months	Yellow shirt, white jumpsuit
Bailey	12 months	Red shirt, plaid overalls
Katherine	18 months	Blue shirt, blue striped overalls
Ben	21 months	White print shirt, tan pants
Sophie	2 1/2 years	Blond hair, red patterned sweater, plaid shirt
Emily	3 years	Pink, blue, and green striped dress
Zacharie	4 years	White shirt, black pants
Alison	4 years	Blond hair, green dress
Stephen	4 1/2 years	Brown shirt with picture of deer, brown pants
Zacharie	4 years	White shirt with pictures of tractors
Emily	6 years	Pigtails, pink bows in hair, blue shirt
Victor	7 years	White, short-sleeved T-shirt
Liesl	7 years	Long dark hair, white and flowered shirt

• Children at Thomas Metcalf School, Illinois State University, kindergarten and elementary classrooms
• Adolescents in social studies and math classes, University High School, Illinois State University
• Children at Goodwood Children's Centre, suburban Adelaide, South Australia, 1- and 2-year-olds

SUMMARY

    Piaget's cognitive-developmental and Vygotsky's sociocultural theories are the focus of this section. After a brief review of Piaget's stages and his view of the child as an active seeker of knowledge, major Piagetian milestones are illustrated. These include development of object permanence in infancy; rapid changes in representation during the second year (including emergence of categorization and make-believe play); gains in ability to conserve, seriate, and categorize flexibly from early to middle childhood; and emergence of hypothetico-deductive reasoning and propositional thought in adolescence. Vygotsky's emphasis on social dialogues as a major source of cognitive development is depicted through images of children working on tasks within their zone of proximal development, engaging private speech, and interacting with adults and peers in ways that promote transfer of culturally adaptive strategies from more expert partners to the child.

MASTERING COURSE CONTENT

Piaget's Cognitive-Developmental Theory

1. The narrator comments, "In the early months of life, infants have some understanding of object permanence." Describe research evidence that supports this claim. (227–228)

_____
_____
_____
_____

2. If 5-month-old Alex has some understanding of *object permanence,* what explains his failure to search for a hidden object? (228) _____

3. Describe three object-hiding tasks in order of difficulty, and indicate whether 8-month-old Randy, 12-month-old Bailey, and 18-month-old Katherine master them at typical ages. (225, Table 6.1)

A. _____ Randy: _____
B. _____ Bailey: _____
C. _____ Katherine: _____

4. What does categorization, illustrated by Katherine's object-sorting, indicate about the development of representation during the first 2 years? Was Piaget correct that representation is the culmination of sensorimotor development? Explain your answer. (230–231)

A. _____
_____
B. _____
_____

5. Compare 18-month-old Katherine's and 21-month-old Ben's make-believe play with that of Stephen and Alison, who are 4 years old. Cite at least three ways in which Stephen's and Alison's make-believe is more advanced. (236)

A. _____
B. _____
C. _____

6. Four-year-old Stephen gives a typical preoperational response to a conservation of liquid task. According to Piaget, which of the following aspects of thinking are indicated by Stephen's failure to conserve? (240–241)

____ lack of object permanence   ____ operational reasoning
____ perception-bound thought   ____ irreversibility
____ centration   ____ lack of categorization

7. Cite three characteristics of concrete operational reasoning illustrated by 7-year-old Victor's response to a conservation of mass problem, and indicate how Victor's explanation portrays each characteristic. (249)

A. _____

B. _____

C. _____

8. Research shows that when tasks are made relevant to their everyday lives, preschoolers do better on Piagetian tasks than expected. How does 4-year-old Alison's performance on a conservation of mass problem illustrate this finding? (245)

_____
_____
_____
_____

9. When given a class inclusion task, what does 7-year-old Victor say that indicates he grasps the idea of hierarchical classification? (249)

_____
_____
_____
_____

10. Describe what distinguishes 4-year-old Stephen's less mature performance from 6-year-old Emily's more mature performance on a seriation task? (249–250)

_____
_____
_____
_____

11. How do the fourth-grade children engaged in a math activity in which they must purchase food items for a family of pigs depict major characteristics of Piaget's concrete operational stage? (249) _____

_____
_____
_____

12. According to Piaget, adolescents become capable of abstract thinking. Describe the two main features of the formal operational stage depicted in the Observation Program. (254)

A. _____
_____

B. _____
_____

13. Describe research that supports the narrator's conclusion that schooling contributes greatly to the development of formal operational thought. (256)

_____
_____
_____

Vygotsky's Sociocultural Theory

14. The Observation Program illustrates Vygotsky's view of cognitive development through images of teachers communicating with pupils and pupils communicating with one another. Why are these images appropriate? (259–260)

_____
_____
_____
_____

15. Several children in the Observation Program use *private speech*. What tasks are they working on, and why do those tasks evoke private speech? According to Vygotsky, what function does private speech serve? (260)

A. _____

_____

B. _____

_____

16. Describe the difference between Piaget's and Vygotsky's views of the development of private speech. Cite three research findings that favor Vygotsky's interpretation. (260)

_____
_____
_____

A. _____
B. _____
C. _____

17. To illustrate the concept of *scaffolding,* 7-month-old Hannah's mother, Connie, demonstrates how a jack-in-the-box works, and 3-year-old Emily put shapes in a container while her mother, Jane, supports her efforts. What is meant by scaffolding? Why does Connie demonstrate, whereas Jane grants Emily the opportunity to perform the task on her own? (261)

A. _____

B. _____

_____

18. According to Vygotsky, to promote cognitive development, collaboration of more expert partners with children should take place on tasks within the *zone of proximal development*. Explain what this means. Are the tasks that Hannah and Emily attempt with the assistance of their mothers within each child's zone of proximal development? Why do you think so? (261)

A. _____

_____

B. _____

_____
_____

19. Watch Professor Berk scaffold 21-month-old Zachary's participation in an imaginative tea party. Next, notice how 4-year-old Alison's father, Larry, *scaffolds* her creation of a tea party. How does scaffolding of make-believe play differ for the two children? Describe the consequences of adult involvement in young children's pretending. (264)

A. _____

_____

_____

_____

_____

B. _____

_____

20. According to Vygotsky, make-believe play leads development forward in two ways. Briefly summarize each. (262)

A. _____

_____

B. _____

_____

21. Is Sophie's father, Kevin, effective at extending her make-believe play with the teddy bear? Explain. How is scaffolding during make-believe different from scaffolding on a task with a single solution, such as putting shapes in a container or working a puzzle?

A. _____

_____

B. _____

_____

_____

BUILDING CONNECTIONS

1. Seven-year-old Liesl's flexible ability to sort a set of shapes in more than one way has implications for her understanding of social categories. Look ahead to Chapter 13, and read the box on page 525. Explain why Liesl is less likely to endorse gender stereotypes (such as "girls aren't good at baseball") than is a younger child like Zacharie, who is a one-dimensional classifier.

_____
_____
_____
_____
_____
_____
_____
_____

2. Summarize the functions of make-believe play recognized by Piaget and Vygotsky (see Chapter 6, pages 237, 262). In view of these functions, how does make-believe support not just cognitive development, but emotional and social development as well?

A. _____
_____
_____
_____
_____

B. _____
_____
_____
_____
_____
_____
_____

3. Piaget's theory has inspired research into many aspects of children's development. Select two of the following: self-concept (Chapter 11, page 445–447); perspective taking (Chapter 11, page 464–466); friendship (Chapter 11, page 468–469); moral reasoning (Chapter 12, page 495–496). Explain how changes from early childhood to adolescence reflect cognitive advances, as described by Piaget.

A. _____
_____
_____
_____
_____

B. _____
_____
_____
_____
_____
_____

APPLYING YOUR KNOWLEDGE:
LEARNING ACTIVITIES

1. Try the object-hiding tasks illustrated in the Observation Program with four infants and toddlers, one from each of the following age ranges: 5–8 months, 8–12 months, 12–18 months, and 18–24 months. Describe each child's behavior, and indicate whether your observations support Piaget's developmental sequence of object permanence. (To review the object-hiding tasks, consult Chapter 6, pages 225–227.)

5–8-month-old _____

_____

8–12-month old _____

_____

12–18-month-old _____

_____

18–24-month-old _____

_____

_____

_____

_____

_____

_____

2. Select two of the following Piagetian tasks illustrated in the Observation Program: conservation (liquid or mass); seriation; class inclusion. Administer the tasks to two children, one 4–5 years, one 6–8 years. Be sure to ask each child for a justification of his or her responses—"How come you think so?" or "Can you explain that to me?" For the younger child, after giving the task in the usual way, try relating it to the child's daily experiences. How does the performance of the younger child differ from that of the older child? Did the younger child's performance improve when you made the task relevant to everyday life? (To review the tasks, consult Chapter 6, page 242 for conservation; page 249–250 for seriation; and page 243 for class inclusion.)

4–5-year-old _____

_____

_____

_____

_____

_____

_____

6–8-year-old _____

_____

_____

_____

_____

_____

_____

_____

3. Contact a child-care center and ask to observe a group of 2- or 3-year-olds during free play for a 30-minute period. How much time do children spend in make-believe play? Do adults in the center often join in children's make-believe, scaffolding it to a more advanced level? Describe instances in which children engage in pretending (a) by themselves, (b) with peers, and (c) with adults. How do make-believe episodes change in duration and complexity across these contexts?

_____
_____
_____
_____
_____
_____
_____
_____
_____
_____
_____
_____
_____
_____
_____
_____
_____

4. Ask a parent to help his or her preschool or school-age child with a challenging task—for example, tying shoes or working a puzzle for the preschooler; a homework assignment for the school-age child. Alternatively, observe a teacher helping a child with a similar task in a preschool or elementary school classroom. Record the adult–child interaction and the child's performance. Does the dialogue have features that support children's mastery? Identify those features and relate them to the Vygotsky-inspired concept of *scaffolding*.

_____
_____
_____
_____
_____
_____
_____
_____
_____
_____
_____
_____
_____
_____
_____
_____

CHAPTER 7

INFORMATION PROCESSING

PARTICIPANTS

Child	Age	To identify on video, look for . . .
Nicole	11 months	White bow in hair, pink and white playsuit
Alison	4 years	Blond hair, green dress
Stephen	4 1/2 years	Brown shirt with picture of deer, brown pants
Zacharie	4 years	White shirt with pictures of tractors
Matthew	4 years	Curly hair, glasses, yellow shirt, navy blue pants
Victor	7 years	White, short-sleeved T-shirt

• Children at Thomas Metcalf School, Illinois State University, kindergarten and elementary classrooms
• Adolescents at University High School, Illinois State University, social studies and math classes

SUMMARY

This section begins by highlighting the concern of information-processing researchers with precise descriptions of children's thinking, often through a computer metaphor. Because memory is crucially important for all kinds of thinking, emphasis is placed on the development of various aspects of remembering. As 4-year-old Stephen and 7-year-old Victor play a memory game, they demonstrate that recognition is ahead of recall. Victor's comments reveal the development of memory strategies and metacognition in middle childhood. As Larry and Linda's discussion of a recent trip to the zoo with Stephen and Alison illustrates, preschoolers' memory in everyday contexts is often excellent, particularly for unusual events. Applications of information processing to literacy and mathematical development are depicted through visits to Metcalf School classrooms and through 4-year-old Matthew's rendition of the story of Little Red Riding Hood. Special attention is given to young children's acquisition of literacy knowledge through play and to major controversies in early reading and mathematics instruction.

TAPE LOG
To view this section, cue tape to: 00:47:25.

MASTERING COURSE CONTENT

Memory Development

1. Compare 4-year-old Stephen and 7-year-old Victor's performance on a game in which each child is asked to remember as many pictures belonging to several categories (vehicles, beach toys, and animals) as he can. According to your text, what explains the improvement in recall memory from the preschool into the school years? (288–290)

_____
_____
_____

2. Review Stephen and Victor's performance on the memory game again. Do either of the children group items together in memory? (To find out, observe the order in which they recall the items.) At about what age do children deliberately engage in such item-grouping? What memory strategy does it suggest? (288–289)

_____
_____
_____
_____

3. Drawing on your knowledge of working memory and long-term memory, explain why the strategy just mentioned helps children recall more items. (273, 289–290)

_____
_____
_____

4. Explain why Stephen's *recognition* in the memory game is considerably more accurate than his *recall?* (291–292)

_____
_____
_____
_____
_____

5. Preschoolers' performance on memory tasks requiring retention of discrete bits of information is similar to that of people in non-Western cultures who have no formal schooling. How does this resemblance shed light on young children's failure to apply memory strategies spontaneously, even after instruction? Why does deliberate use of memory strategies accompany formal schooling? (290)

A. _____
_____
_____

B. _____
_____
_____

6. Victor has substantial *metacognitive knowledge* about how to remember. Describe what he knows, and explain why metacognition is likely to help Victor when he is faced with a recall task. (300–301)

_____
_____
_____
_____
_____
_____

7. Record the information Stephen and Alison remember about a special one-time event—a trip to the zoo. Is their recall for everyday experiences likely to be better than their memory for listlike information? Explain your answer. (290)

A. _____
_____
_____

B. _____
_____
_____
_____

8. Explain why Stephen and Alison's recall of a one-time event is likely to be more detailed than their recall of a familiar experience (one that happens every day or several times a week)? In what form do young children recall familiar experiences? Why is this form of memory useful? (295–297)

A. _____
_____
_____

B. _____
_____
_____

C. _____
_____
_____

9. In talking with their son and daughter about past events, how are Larry and Linda helping Stephen and Alison build an autobiographical memory? (296–297)

_____
_____
_____
_____
_____

10. As Stephen and Alison get older, they will be unlikely to recall experiences that happened to them before age 3. What is this type of forgetting called? _____ According to a growing number of researchers, what two developmental milestones bring an end to this period of forgetting? (296)

A. _____

B. _____

Applications of Information Processing to Academic Learning

11. In the Illinois State University Child Care Center, reading to young children is a daily activity. What does research say about its contribution to literacy development and later academic performance? (305)

_____
_____
_____
_____
_____
_____
_____
_____
_____

12. Will 4-year-old Matthew's storytelling ability be an asset when he receives formal instruction in reading after beginning elementary school? Explain. (304–305)

_____
_____
_____
_____
_____

13. Why is Matthew's memory for the story of Little Red Riding Hood so rich and elaborate? What type of memory is Matthew demonstrating? (292–293)

_____
_____
_____
_____
_____

14. Describe some of the ways the recycling center in Metcalf School's kindergarten prepares children for reading? Why are young children likely to pick up more literacy knowledge in this play activity than through formal instruction in letters and sounds? (304–305)

A. _____
_____
_____
_____

B. _____
_____
_____
_____
_____

15. Describe the "great debate" over teaching beginning reading. Why do some

44

experts advocate a balanced mixture of both approaches? (305)

A. _____

_____

_____

B. _____

_____

_____

_____

_____

_____

16. How does the lesson in the whole-language classroom at Metcalf School illustrate basic assumptions of this approach to teaching beginning reading? (305)

_____

_____

_____

_____

17. Availability of informal counting experiences in children's everyday lives promotes early number understandings. As kindergartners play in the recycling center, they reveal their grasp of basic mathematical principles. Name these, and describe the behaviors that illustrate each. (306)

_____

_____

_____

_____

18. Arguments about how best to teach mathematics—through stressing math-fact retrieval or "number sense"—resemble opposing viewpoints in reading. How does the fifth-grade math lesson in the Observation Program depict a blend of both approaches? (307)

_____

_____

_____

_____

BUILDING CONNECTIONS

1. Metacognitive knowledge is important not just for cognitive problem solving, but for social competence as well. Look ahead to Chapter 11, pages 472–474, and read the section on social problem solving. What do children have to be *aware of* to solve social problems effectively?

_____
_____
_____
_____
_____

2. Your text indicates that although metacognitive knowledge increases with age, school-age children do not always apply what they know about mental activity to improve their performance. What does Vygotsky's theory suggest about how to foster self-regulation? Why is it important to offer children explanations for the effectiveness of self-regulatory strategies? (See Chapter 7, page 302.)

_____
_____
_____
_____
_____
_____

3. When parents take time to talk about past experiences (as Larry and Linda did with Stephen and Alison), they help their children construct an autobiographical memory. What emotional and social competencies might they also be fostering through conversations about the past?

_____
_____
_____
_____
_____
_____
_____
_____

4. What content makes Matthew's rendition of the story of Little Red Riding Hood more typical of a boy's than a girl's retelling? What themes would a girl be more likely to emphasize? (Chapter 13, page 548, 550–551.)

_____
_____
_____
_____
_____
_____
_____
_____
_____

5. Read the box in Chapter 7 on page 308 (Asian Children's Understanding of Multidigit Addition and Subtraction) and the box in Chapter 15 on page 638 (Education in Japan, Taiwan, and the United States). What supports for academic learning do Asian children receive that are not widely available to American children?

_____
_____
_____
_____
_____
_____
_____
_____
_____

APPLYING YOUR KNOWLEDGE:
LEARNING ACTIVITIES

1. Using stickers or pictures from magazines, prepare the materials needed for the memory game illustrated in the Observation Program and try it with a 4- to 6-year-old child. Note the child's recall score. Then embed the need to remember in a meaningful context. For example, ask the child to play shopkeeper, and indicate that it is important to recall all the items for sale in the store. Did the child's memory improve? Did he or she use any strategies to aid recall?

_____
_____
_____
_____
_____
_____
_____

2. Interview a 5- to 6-year-old and a 7- to 9-year-old for knowledge of memory strategies, using the following questions as well as one or two that you make up yourself.

A. When you try to remember things, do you remember some things better than others? What kinds of things are hard to remember? Which ones are easier to remember?
B. Suppose I wanted you to remember some pictures. I give you 3 minutes to look at them, and then I take them away. What would you do to learn the pictures?
C. Suppose I tell you a story and ask you to remember it. Would it be easier to remember it word for word or in your own words? Why?

Describe each child's responses:

5- to 6-year-old _____
_____
_____
_____

7- to 9-year-old _____
_____
_____
_____

Did metacognitive knowledge increase with age? What factors—internal to the child and in the child's experiences—probably contribute to the development of metacognition during this age period?

_____
_____
_____
_____
_____
_____

Applying Your Knowledge: Learning Activities (continued)

3. Arrange to observe several periods of academic instruction in an elementary school classroom. Cite examples of how the teacher promotes each of the following aspects of information processing:

use of memory strategies _____
_____
_____
_____
_____

metacognitive knowledge _____
_____
_____
_____
_____

self-regulation _____
_____
_____
_____
_____

basic reading and mathematical skills _____
_____
_____
_____
_____

reading comprehension and/or appreciation of the uses of mathematics _____
_____
_____
_____
_____

What position does the teacher seem to take on the debates described in the text about how to teach beginning reading and mathematics? (See pages 305 and 307.)
_____
_____
_____
_____
_____

CHAPTER 8

INTELLIGENCE

PARTICIPANTS

• Children at Thomas Metcalf School, Illinois State University, kindergarten through eighth grade
• Angela and Mary, art educators, and children and adolescents in Access Arts, an after-school art education program in suburban Adelaide, Australia

SUMMARY

This section opens by emphasizing the controversy among psychologists and educators over the meaning and usefulness of IQ scores. Howard Gardner's theory of multiple intelligences is highlighted to depict the diversity of human mental abilities, not all of which are represented on current tests. A fourth-grade class in which many learning activities are organized around Gardner's multiple intelligences is shown. Next, the Observation Program returns to the children's circus to illustrate training of bodily/kinesthetic abilities. The circus also provides the context for discussing the many factors that contribute to development of creativity and special talents.

```
TAPE LOG
To view this section, cue tape to: 00:57:52.
```

MASTERING COURSE CONTENT

1. The narrator comments that debate among psychologists and educators about the meaning and usefulness of IQ scores is intense. Describe the following differences of opinion:

A. Intelligence as holistic or multifaceted (316–317) _____
_____
_____

B. Intelligence as independent of or sensitive to environmental contexts (321–322)
_____
_____

C. Intelligence as a set of interrelated or distinct, independent skills (317–318, 321–322)
_____
_____

2. Cite the most recent theory to take a balanced position on the holistic versus multifaceted controversy by proposing a hierarchical model of intelligence. (319–320)

_____

3. What statistical procedure was used to devise this as well as other hierarchical models of intelligence? (317) _____

4. What theory emphasizes the sensitivity of intelligence to environmental contexts? (321–322) _____

5. What theory proposes eight distinct, independent intelligences? (322–323)

_____

6. Which of the following of Gardner's intelligences are represented on currently available tests for children? Which are not represented? (322)

Yes/No	Linguistic	Yes/No	Bodily/Kinesthetic
Yes/No	Logico-mathematical	Yes/No	Naturalist
Yes/No	Musical	Yes/No	Interpersonal
Yes/No	Spatial	Yes/No	Intrapersonal

7. Review the visit to the fourth-grade class, in which many learning activities are organized around Gardner's multiple intelligences. Children take on different roles from one assignment to the next, with the goal of fostering many mental abilities. In an assignment in which children use clues to figure out the meaning of novel symbols, indicate which intelligences are promoted by each of the following roles: (323)

Recorder _____

Problem solver _____

Encourager _____

8. The narrator points out that besides bodily/kinesthetic intelligence, the children's circus fosters interpersonal intelligence. Cite examples of children's behaviors that demonstrate this. (323)

_____
_____
_____
_____

9. Listen to Angela and Mary, art educators, describe the program at Access Arts. Which of the following theoretical views of creativity does Access Arts illustrate? (350–351)
       _____ The psychometric view   _____ A multifaceted view

Explain, citing ingredients of creativity mentioned by Angela and Mary.

_____
_____
_____

10. Name one influential multifaceted approach to creativity. (351)

_____

11. According to Sternberg and Lubart, creativity is a product of cognitive, personality, motivational, and environmental resources. Cite specific ways that Access Arts encourages each. (351–353)

Cognitive resources _____

_____

Personality resources _____

_____

Motivational resources _____

_____

Environmental resources _____

_____

BUILDING CONNECTIONS

1. In the children's circus at Metcalf School, cooperative learning and multigrade instruction are used to promote children's learning. Older, more expert pupils assist younger, novice pupils in acquiring new bodily/kinesthetic competencies. What theory of cognitive development is consistent with this approach to instruction? Explain your answer. (If you have difficulty, return to Chapter 6, page 263–266.)

_____
_____
_____
_____
_____

2. In cooperative learning and multigrade instruction, younger pupils benefit through mastery of new skills. How do older pupils benefit, academically, emotionally, and socially? (See Chapter 15, page 613, 633–634)

_____
_____
_____
_____
_____
_____
_____
_____
_____

3. How does Access Arts promote self-esteem and a mastery-oriented approach to learning in children? (See Chapter 11, pages 451–456)

_____
_____
_____
_____
_____
_____
_____
_____
_____
_____
_____
_____
_____
_____
_____

APPLYING YOUR KNOWLEDGE:

LEARNING ACTIVITIES

1. Suppose that children's intelligence is assessed in the following two situations: (a) using a standardized intelligence test in their elementary school classroom and (b) on the basis of their performance over time in the children's circus? To what extent are the two assessments likely to be correlated? How well is each assessment likely to predict scholastic performance? How about later life success? Explain your answers.

_____
_____
_____
_____
_____
_____
_____
_____
_____
_____
_____
_____
_____
_____
_____
_____
_____
_____
_____
_____
_____

2. The narrator comments that no matter how natively gifted, any child can participate in the children's circus. What characteristics of the circus learning environment grant low-income and ethnic minority children the opportunity to excel, whereas they typically fall behind their middle-class peers in traditional academic contexts?

_____
_____
_____
_____
_____
_____
_____
_____
_____
_____
_____
_____
_____
_____
_____
_____
_____

Applying Your Knowledge: Learning Activities (continued)

3. According to Sternberg and Lubart's investment theory of creativity, many people can develop creativity to varying degrees. Home and school environments need to support its development by helping new ideas form and develop. Select one of the following activities:

A. Provide advice to parents who want to nurture their child's creativity and special talents. What general approaches to child rearing should parents adopt? Describe research findings that support your recommendations. (See Chapter 8, page 352–353.)

_____
_____
_____
_____
_____
_____
_____
_____
_____
_____
_____
_____
_____
_____

B. Provide advice to teachers who want to nurture their pupils' creativity and special talents. What general approaches to instruction should teachers adopt? How do Angela and Mary use those techniques? Describe research findings that support your recommendations?

_____
_____
_____
_____
_____
_____
_____
_____
_____
_____
_____
_____
_____

(For assistance with this activity, consult Chapter 8, pages 352–353; Chapter 11, pages 454–456; Chapter 14, pages 563; and Chapter 15, pages 627, 632–634.)

CHAPTER 9

LANGUAGE DEVELOPMENT

PARTICIPANTS

Child	Age	To identify on video, look for ...
Anna Marie	2 weeks	White long-sleeved shirt and diaper, white socks
Cara	6 weeks	White, short-sleeved suit, bare legs and feet; later, pink sleep suit
Mac	3 months	Red shirt, blue overalls
Alex	5 months	Green playsuit
Hannah	7 months	Pink bow on head, multicolored playsuit with pink top
Nicole	11 months	White bow in hair, pink and white playsuit
Katherine	18 months	Blue shirt, blue striped overalls
Ben	21 months	White print shirt, tan pants
Zachary	23 months	Green, black, and white striped shirt
Alison	4 years	Blond hair, green dress
Joshua	5 years	Blue shirt, red pants

• Children and teachers at Thomas Metcalf Laboratory School, kindergarten and elementary classrooms, and at the Child Care Center, Illinois State University

SUMMARY

Is language biologically programmed, the result of parental teaching, or due to the combined influence of innate endowment and a rich linguistic and social environment? Theoretical debate over how young children acquire language introduces this section. Prelinguistic development is depicted through examples of infant receptivity to language and characteristics of parent–infant interaction that help infants make sense of a complex speech stream. Alex, Hannah, Zachary, Katherine, and Nicole demonstrate early communicative capacities, first words in the second year of life, and the distinction between language comprehension and production. Zachary and Ben highlight individual differences in early styles of language learning. Preschoolers and kindergartners playing and conversing display remarkable linguistic attainments in semantics, grammar, and pragmatics by the end of early childhood. The importance of adult–child interaction for stimulating language progress is emphasized.

> ## TAPE LOG
> To view this section, cue tape to: 1:05:26.

MASTERING COURSE CONTENT

1. Briefly describe the behaviorist and nativist perspectives on language development. For each, note supportive evidence and limitations. (359–365)

Behaviorist _____

_____

Supportive evidence _____

_____

Limitations _____

_____

Nativist

_____

_____

Supportive evidence _____

_____

_____

Limitations _____

_____

2. Which well-known psychologist originated the behaviorist perspective on language development? (359)

_____

Which well-known linguist originated the nativist perspective on language development? (359)

_____

3. Describe the interactionist perspective on language development, noting limitations and unresolved issues. (3464–366)

_____
_____
_____
_____

4. Cite at least two examples from the Observation Program that illustrate the joint contribution of inner predispositions and environmental inputs to language development. (364–366)

A. _____

_____

B. _____

_____

5. Observe 2-week-old Anna Marie; 6-week-old Cara; and 3-month-old Mac interacting with their mothers. Describe evidence indicating that Anna Marie, Cara, and Mac are sensitive to a wider range of speech sounds than are older infants, children, and adults. (367)

_____
_____
_____
_____
_____

6. The narrator comments that over the first year, infants detect word and phrase units that are crucial for making sense of the language they hear. Summarize evidence that supports this statement. (367)

_____
_____
_____
_____

7. Listen as 7-month-old Hannah's mother, Connie, speaks to her. What term is used to describe the form of language Connie uses? _____
List characteristics of this form of language, and explain why adults use it when talking to infants. (367)

_____
_____
_____

8. The text points out that parents constantly fine-tune their child-directed speech, adjusting the length and content of their utterances to fit with children's needs. Note how 18-month-old Katherine's parents interact with her. How does their communication differ from that of 7-month-old Hannah's mother? (368)

_____
_____
_____
_____

9. Listen to Hannah's babbling. Cite two ways in which babbling paves the way for language. (368)
A. _____
B. _____

10. Zachary uses a preverbal gesture when he points, then adds the word "ball." What is his gesture called? (369)

_____

11. Nicole and Zachary illustrate how language comprehension is ahead of production. Explain why. (372)

_____

12. One of 23-month-old Zachary's first words is "ball." What makes this a typical word in children's early vocabularies? (372, 375)

_____
_____

13. Explain how Zachary and Ben's personalities contribute to different rates of vocabulary growth. Observe Zachary's and Ben's mothers interacting with each of them. How might parental speech influence individual differences in language progress? (374)

_____
_____

14. Using the kindergartner reading a story, the preschool boys conversing during block play, 5-year-old Josh "talking down" to his baby sister Hannah, and Alison's polite way of saying it's time to go, cite examples of children's semantic, grammatical, and pragmatic competencies by the end of the preschool years.
Semantics (373, 375–376)

_____

_____
_____
_____

Grammar (380–383) _____

_____
_____
_____

Pragmatics (386–389)

_____

_____
_____
_____

15. Drawing on examples of teachers interacting with young children in the Observation Program, explain why adult–child conversation is so important for language development in early childhood? (386)

_____
_____
_____

BUILDING CONNECTIONS

1. Look ahead to Chapter 10, page 426, and read the section on quality of caregiving and security of attachment. Then review the examples of parents communicating with their babies in the Observation Program. How does child-directed speech contribute to the development of a secure attachment bond?

_____
_____
_____
_____
_____

2. Look closely at 5-year-old Joshua adjusting his speech to fit the age of his baby sister Hannah. What does Joshua's behavior indicate about the validity of Piaget's conclusion that preschoolers are egocentric? (See Chapter 6, page 240.)

_____
_____
_____
_____

3. Your text and the Observation Program emphasize that opportunities to converse with adults are consistently related to general measures of language progress. How might this finding help explain socioeconomic (SES) differences in intelligence test performance and academic achievement? (See Chapter 14, page 568 for a description of SES differences in styles of child rearing.)

_____
_____
_____
_____
_____
_____

4. In view of the role of adult–child communication in language development, why are group size, caregiver–child ratio, and caregiver educational preparation vital ingredients of quality in preschool and child-care settings? (See Chapter 14, page 586.)

_____
_____
_____
_____
_____

5. Why did Vygotsky regard language, and the resulting ability to engage in social dialogues with others, as especially significant in children's development? (See Chapter 6, pages 260–262.)

_____
_____
_____
_____

APPLYING YOUR KNOWLEDGE:
LEARNING ACTIVITIES

1. Your text points out that native endowment, cognitive development, and social experience may operate in different balances with respect to each component of language. Indicate your view of the relative importance of each factor for semantic, grammatical, and pragmatic development, and justify your position with research evidence.

Semantic Development

____ Native endowment ____ Cognitive development ____ Social experience

Research evidence _____
_____
_____
_____

Grammatical Development

____ Native endowment ____ Cognitive development ____ Social experience

Research evidence _____
_____
_____
_____

Pragmatic Development

____ Native endowment ____ Cognitive development ____ Social experience

Research evidence _____
_____
_____
_____

2. Interview a parent of a child between 18 and 24 months of age, asking for a list of the words the child produces and the contexts in which each is used. Look for illustrations of the sensorimotor foundations of early language, the spurt in vocabulary that often occurs around this time, and first two-word combinations.
_____
_____
_____
_____
_____
_____
_____
_____
_____

Applying Your Knowledge: Learning Activities (continued)

3. Observe a child between 2 and 5 years of age for a 30-minute period, and record all of the child's utterances. Examine the language sample for each of the following features:

A. Number of different words spoken _____
B. Percentage of words that are object words _____ action words _____ state (or modifier) words _____
C. Examples of overextensions _____
D. Average length of sentences (in number of words) _____
E. Examples of complex grammatical constructions _____
_____
_____
_____

Compare your findings with those of several of your classmates for documentation of rapid language development in early childhood.
_____
_____
_____
_____
_____
_____
_____
_____
_____
_____
_____
_____
_____

CHAPTER 10

EMOTIONAL DEVELOPMENT

PARTICIPANTS

Child	Age	To identify on video, look for ...
Anna Marie	2 weeks	White, long-sleeved shirt and diaper, white socks
Cara	6 weeks	White, short-sleeved suit, bare legs and feet; later, pink sleep suit
Mac	3 months	Red shirt, blue overalls
Alex	5 months	Green playsuit
Hannah	7 months	Pink bow on head, multicolored playsuit with pink top
Randy	8 months	Yellow shirt, white jumpsuit
Nicole	11 months	White bow in hair, pink and white playsuit
Bailey	12 months	Red shirt, plaid overalls
Braxton	15 months	White shirt, black pants
Katherine	18 months	Blue shirt, blue striped overalls
Ben	21 months	White print shirt, tan pants
Zachary	23 months	Green, black, and white striped shirt
Kristin	3 1/2 years	White bow in hair, plaid playsuit
Alison	4 years	Blond hair, green dress
Stephen	4 1/2 years	Brown shirt with picture of deer, brown pants
Zacharie	4 years	White shirt with pictures of tractors
Joshua	5 years	Blue shirt, red pants

SUMMARY

The role of emotions in organizing and regulating many aspects of experience is underscored in this section. Emotional milestones of infancy—the social smile, laughter, fear (including stranger anxiety), use of the caregiver as a secure base, and social referencing—are illustrated. Then the Observation Program focuses on temperament. Individual differences in sociability, attention span, activity level, and persistence are shown, and the importance of adapting parenting to children's temperamental styles is emphasized. Next, the development of infant–caregiver attachment is considered. Among the milestones depicted are newborn capacities that evoke loving care; emotional responsiveness to the familiar caregiver in the first half year; appearance of clear-cut attachment (including separation anxiety) around 6 to 8 months; and the capacity to tolerate short parental absences by the end of the second year. The vital role of sensitive, responsive care in the development of a secure attachment bond is explained. The section concludes with similarities and differences in mothers' and fathers' styles of interacting with their babies.

MASTERING COURSE CONTENT

Emotional Development in Infancy and Toddlerhood

1. Review the images of Zach, Alex, Randy, Ben, Nicole, and Kristin at the beginning of this section. Describe the emotions each expresses, and indicate how that emotion helps organize and regulate behavior. (398–399)

Zach (with jack-in-the-box) _____

_____

Alex (watching toy) _____

_____

Randy (watching Ben) _____

_____

Ben (playing ball) _____

_____

Kristin and Nicole (playing ball) _____

_____

_____

2. Which approach to emotional development takes the view that emotions are central, adaptive forces in all aspects of human activity? (398)

_____

3. Describe Bonnie's reaction to Cara's social smile in the Observation Program. What role does the social smile play in the parent–infant relationship and the baby's developing competence? (402)
A. _____

_____

B. _____

_____

4. Describe the events that make 7-month-old Hannah and 23-month-old Zachary laugh. How do the two events differ? What explains this age-related change in the circumstances that evoke laughter? (402)
Hannah _____
Zachary _____

_____

_____

5. When do fear reactions appear in infancy, and why are they adaptive? (403)

_____

_____

_____

6. Eight-month-old Randy displays *stranger anxiety*. What three factors affect an infant's fear of unfamiliar adults? (403)
A. _____

B. _____

C. _____

7. Review Randy's expression of stranger anxiety again. What can a parent do to ease it? What can an unfamiliar adult do? (403)

A. _____

B. _____

8. What is meant by a *secure base?* What behaviors indicate that Randy uses Sheryl as a secure base? (403)

_____

_____

9. Randy engages in *social referencing.* Explain this behavior, and indicate why it develops by the end of the first year. (408–409)

_____

_____

_____

10. What does social referencing reveal about infants' emotional understanding? (408–409)

_____

_____

_____

Temperament and Development

11. One way of assessing temperament is through direct observation. Describe behaviors of children in the Observation Program that suggest the following temperamental characteristics: (414–415)

Shy (Zachary) _____

Sociable (Katherine) _____

Attentive (Stephen and Alison) _____

Distractible (Zacharie) _____

Inactive, cautious (Stephen and Alison) _____

Active, willing to take risks (Zacharie) _____

Persistent (Zachary) _____

Easily frustrated (Braxton) _____

12. Explain *goodness of fit.* How does Joanna's enthusiastic response to Braxton's success with the box of shapes create a "good fit" with his temperament and encourage more adaptive functioning?

A. _____

_____

B. _____

_____

69

Development of Attachment

13. What theory of attachment takes into account babies' behaviors that evoke care and attention from adults? (422)

_____

14. Observe 2-week-old Anna Marie, 6-week-old Alex, and 7-month-old Hannah interacting with caregivers. For each, describe behaviors that serve to keep the caregiver nearby. (422)

Anna Marie _____

_____

_____

Alex _____

_____

_____

Hannah _____

_____

_____

15. According to Bowlby, the development of attachment takes place in four phases. Note behaviors of Anna Marie, Alex, Hannah, and Katherine that reveal the phase of attachment each child has reached. (422–423)

The preattachment phase:
Child _____ Behaviors _____

_____

The "attachment-in-the-making" phase:
Child _____ Behaviors _____

_____

The phase of "clear-cut" attachment:
Child _____ Behaviors _____

_____

Formation of a reciprocal relationship:
Child _____ Behaviors _____

_____

16. In the Observation Program, Katherine's parents leave the room, and Katherine remains with an unfamiliar adult (Professor Berk). What technique for measuring the quality of attachment does this resemble? (423–424)

_____

17. According to your text and the Observation Program, _____ care supports the development of attachment. Describe caregiving behaviors of parents in the Observation Program that foster attachment security. (426)

_____

_____

_____

18. Review the temperamental characteristics illustrated earlier in the Observation Program, noting 8-month-old Braxton's irritable, distress-prone behavior. (427–428)

True or False: Braxton's temperament increases the risk of insecure attachment.
True or False: When infant irritability is linked to insecure attachment, temperament (not caregiving) is responsible.
True or False: The influence of temperament on security of attachment depends on goodness-of-fit.

19. Watch parents interacting with their infants and toddlers at the end of this section. How do mothers and fathers differ? (430)

_____

_____

20. Art kisses and cuddles 6-week-old Cara. What factor is particularly important in supporting fathers' involvement with babies? (430)

_____

21. The narrator comments that attachment has far-reaching consequences for children's development. Describe research related to this statement. Is evidence on the long-term consequences of attachment clear? (430–432)

_____

_____

_____

BUILDING CONNECTIONS

1. How do the social smiles of 6-week-old Cara and 3-month-old Alex parallel the development of infant perceptual capacities—in particular, babies' increasing sensitivity to visual patterns, including the human face? (See Chapter 4, pages 159–163.)

_____
_____
_____
_____
_____

2. In Chapter 4 (see page 158–159), research indicating that crawling experience affects fear of depth-at-an-edge is presented. How is this finding consistent with the adaptive value of fearful reactions, discussed in Chapter 10?

_____
_____
_____
_____
_____

3. Research indicates that temperament affects conscience development. Look ahead to Chapter 12, and read the box on page 483. In view of their temperaments, why is it relatively easy for Stephen and Alison's parents to promote moral internalization in their children? Why is it more difficult for Zacharie's mother to do so? Why should Zacharie's mother avoid power assertive discipline? What should she do instead?

A. _____
_____
B. _____
_____
C. _____
_____
_____
_____

4. Select one of the following: self-development (Chapter 11, page 441); moral development (Chapter 12, page 483–484); and peer sociability (Chapter 15, page 599). Look ahead in your text, and read the section on that topic. Summarize the contribution of a secure attachment bond to that aspect of development.

_____
_____
_____
_____
_____
_____
_____

APPLYING YOUR KNOWLEDGE:
LEARNING ACTIVITIES

1. The text indicates that signs of almost all the basic emotions—happiness, interest, surprise, fear, anger, sadness, and disgust—are present in early infancy (see page 401). Review earlier segments of the Observation Program, and carefully observe the facial, body, and vocal expressions of infants of different ages. Record instances of the basic emotions listed above, and compare younger with older babies.

Anna Marie (2 weeks) _____

Cara (6 weeks) _____

Mac (3 months) _____

Alex (5 months) _____

Hannah (7 months) _____

Randy (8 months) _____

Nicole (11 months) _____

Do emotional expressions seem to become better organized and more recognizable with age? _____

2. Review the section on development of emotional self-regulation in the text (see pages 404–405). Return to the Observation Program, and watch mothers and fathers interacting with their infants. Select two examples, and describe how each parent fosters emotional self-regulation. Pay particular attention to the pace of the parents' behavior in relation to the baby's needs.

A. _____
_____
_____
_____
_____
_____

B. _____
_____
_____
_____
_____
_____
_____
_____

3. Arrange to visit a child-care center during early morning hours, when parents bring their infants, toddlers, and young preschoolers for the day. What steps do the staff take to ease the stress of separation from the parent? How do children greet their caregivers? Describe several examples, and indicate whether children seem, for the most part, securely attached to professional caregivers? On the basis of information provided in Table 10.6 on page 435 of the text, rate the overall quality of the child-care center as excellent, average, or poor. Is overall quality related to sensitive, responsive care? Explain.

Steps staff take to ease separation anxiety
_____
_____
_____
_____
_____
_____
_____

Quality of attachment to professional caregivers _____
_____
_____
_____
_____
_____
_____

Overall quality of the child-care center   ___ excellent ___ average ___ poor

Relationship of center quality to sensitive, responsive care _____
_____
_____
_____
_____
_____
_____
_____

CHAPTER 11

SELF AND SOCIAL UNDERSTANDING

PARTICIPANTS

Hannah	7 months	Pink bow on head, multicolored playsuit with pink top
Nicole	11 months	White bow in hair, pink and white playsuit
Ben	21 months	White print shirt, tan pants
Zachary	23 months	Green, black, and white striped shirt
Kristin	3 1/2 years	White bow in hair, plaid playsuit
Emily	4 years	White blouse, pink and purple patterned jumper
Claire	5 years	Blond hair, pink dress
Emily	6 years	Blond pigtails, pink bow in hair, blue shirt
Liesl	7 years	Long dark hair, white and flowered shirt
Victor	7 years	White, short-sleeved T-shirt
Allysa	7 years	Glasses, blue shirt, plaid overalls
Jean	17 years	Black tank top and jeans
Phil	17 years	Tan shirt, mustache and beard
Carla	17 years	Olive green shirt
Mark	24 years	Black and white plaid shirt

• Oscar, Dorothy, and their 8-year-old son Alex
• Wendy Koolmatrie, director, and the children of Kalaya Children's Centre, suburban Adelaide, South Australia

SUMMARY

This section addresses children's understanding of themselves, other people, and relationships between people. Emergence of self-recognition is explored by dabbing red dye on toddlers' noses and observing reactions to their changed appearance using a mirror. The importance of a sense of agency for early self-development is illustrated. During the preschool years, children begin to form a naive theory of mind—a coherent understanding of mental life. Four-year-old Emily's behavior in a game in which she is asked to mislead an adult reveals her understanding of false belief. School-age children's self-descriptions depict the development of self-concept, from concrete characteristics and typical emotions and behaviors to personality traits. Five-year-old Claire and 7-year-old Liesl play a game that reveals gains in perspective taking during the early school years. Children's concepts of friendship are illustrated by their responses to the question, "What makes a good friend?" The importance of social experience—in particular, the guidance of parents and teachers—in children's grasp of interpersonal relations is emphasized.

Jean, Phil, and Carla, seniors at University High School, combine their various personality traits into an organized self-concept and discuss their experiences in constructing an identity. Mark, a college student, looks back on his struggle to formulate a sexual identity in adolescence. A sense of ethnic heritage and belonging is an important dimension of identity. Oscar and Dorothy, parents of 8-year-old Alex, bring together two ethnicities. They discuss their efforts to help Alex learn about and appreciate his rich ethnic heritage. Wendy Koolmatrie, director, Kalaya Children's Centre, describes a program that assists Australian Aboriginal children in constructing a positive ethnic identity beginning in the preschool years.

```
┌─────────────────────────────────────────┐
│              TAPE LOG                     │
│  To view this section, cue tape to: 1:16:19.│
└─────────────────────────────────────────┘
```

MASTERING COURSE CONTENT

1. Compare the reactions of 11-month-old Nicole, 23-month-old Zachary, and 3-year-old Kristin to their changed appearance in a mirror. What behaviors indicate that Zachary and Kristin clearly recognize themselves? (441)

_____
_____
_____

2. Summarize the role of infants' actions in early self-development. (441)

_____
_____
_____

3. The narrator comments that noticing the contrast between reactions of the physical world, the social world, and their own movements may help infants and toddlers build an image of self as separate from external reality. Explain what he means. (441)

_____
_____
_____

4. When asked to trick her mother, what does 4-year-old Emily say and do to indicate her understanding of false belief? (443)

_____
_____
_____
_____

5. Why is preschoolers' mastery of false belief a landmark achievement? (443)

_____
_____

6. List factors that may have contributed to Emily's mastery of false belief. (444–445) _____
_____

7. Four-year-old Emily has an older sister. What does research say about sibling

78

influences on false-belief reasoning? (445)

_____
_____
_____

8. Cite examples of children's self-descriptions depicted in the Observation Program. What makes these typical of the self-concepts of young school-age children? (445)

A. _____
_____
_____

B. _____
_____
_____

9. In contrast to 5-year-old Claire who has a partial understanding, 7-year-old Liesl indicates that neither a child her age nor a baby would be able to identify a picture of a horse from a nondescript part. What does Liesl's reasoning indicate about her perspective-taking skills? (466)

_____
_____
_____

10. How is Liesl's perspective-taking competence likely to help her get along with other people? (466–467)

_____
_____

11. List the three stages of friendship understanding presented in the text. What stage is 7-year-old Liesl at? Explain why. (468–469)

Level 1
_____
Level 2
_____
Level 3
_____

_____
_____
_____
_____
_____
_____

12. Victor realizes that an important ingredient of friendship is common values. List attributes on which friends tend to resemble one another. (470–471)

_____
_____
_____
_____
_____

13. At age 7, Liesl and Victor are advanced in their grasp of the meaning of friendship. How can learning activities in classrooms promote social understanding? What does Allysa's essay reveal about her stage of friendship understanding? (468–469)

A. _____

_____

B. _____

_____

14. How does Jean's description of herself differ from the way grade-school children describe themselves? (447)

_____

_____

_____

15. Phil explains that he is much less concerned about how others view him as a senior than he was when he entered high school. What factors probably contributed to this change? (449)

_____

_____

_____

16. Carla describes some conflict with her parents as she defines her own values. According to the text, what can Carla's parents do to foster identity development? (458–460)

_____

_____

_____

17. Describe factors that made it difficult for Mark to formulate a positive homosexual identity. Then describe conditions that encouraged Mark to "come out"—that is, to be forthright with himself and others about his homosexuality. (Chapter 5, page 213)

A. _____

_____

B. _____

_____

18. Oscar mentions that his 8-year-old son, Alex, focuses on color more than ethnicity in distinguishing people. How is this focus on color typical of children's person perception? (463)

_____

_____

_____

19. Cite ways that Oscar and Dorothy are fostering a sense of ethnic pride in Alex. Are their efforts likely to succeed? Explain. (461)

_____

_____

_____

_____

20. Why is constructing a positive ethnic identity particularly challenging for minority children, such as the Australian Aboriginal children at Kalaya Children's Centre? (461)

_____

_____

_____

_____

21. What steps does Kalaya Children's Centre take to promote a positive ethnic identity among Aboriginal children, as well as contact and respect between ethnic groups? Are the children at Kalaya likely to develop a bicultural identity? Explain. (461)

A. _____

_____

_____

B. _____

_____

_____

BUILDING CONNECTIONS

1. Victor's insightful comment that "bad kids" may become friends and negatively influence one another is borne out by research. Look ahead to the box on page 513 of Chapter 12 and the box on page 614–615 of Chapter 15. Explain the role of deviant peer associations in juvenile delinquency and adolescent substance abuse.

_____
_____
_____
_____
_____
_____
_____
_____
_____
_____
_____
_____
_____
_____

2. Perspective taking is vital for many aspects of social understanding. Return to pages 410–411 of Chapter 10 and reread the section on empathy. Explain how the development of empathy depends on advances in perspective taking.

_____
_____
_____
_____
_____
_____
_____
_____
_____
_____
_____
_____

3. Review the school-age children's self-descriptions and comments about what it means to be a good friend. Notice that children seem to be more advanced in friendship understanding than in self-concept. Recall from Chapters 6 and 7 that children's cognitive development is often uneven across tasks. Why might these children display more mature ideas about friendship than self-perceptions?

_____
_____
_____
_____
_____
_____
_____
_____
_____
_____
_____
_____

Building Connections (continued)

4. Cite evidence from the Observation Program that Alex's father's Mexican-American heritage and the Australian Aboriginal children's heritage is collectivist rather than individualistic? (Chapter 1, page 36.)

A. _____
_____
_____

B. _____
_____
_____

5. Describe common challenges faced by homosexual youths and ethnic minority youths in forging a positive sense of identity. (Chapter 5, page 213; Chapter 11, page 461.)

_____
_____
_____
_____
_____
_____
_____
_____
_____
_____
_____

APPLYING YOUR KNOWLEDGE:
LEARNING ACTIVITIES

1. A parent reports that she took her 3-year-old son Danny to a magic show, and he was amazed that rabbits could come out of hats and pigeons out of coat sleeves. At home, he looked in hats and up coat sleeves to see if animals lived there. A year later, Danny attended another magic show and commented, "Aw, that man's just trying to trick us!" What change in Danny's view of the mind underlies his grasp of magic as trickery? Explain your answer. (If you have difficulty with this question, consult Chapter 11, page 443–444.)

_____
_____
_____

2. Interview two children—a preschooler and a school-age child—to explore their self-concepts. Begin by asking a general question, such as "Tell me about yourself." Then follow up with more specific queries addressing children's likes and dislikes and beliefs about their own competencies (for example, "What do you think you are good at and not good at?") Take notes on children's responses. What did each emphasize: name, physical appearance, everyday emotions and behaviors) or personality traits?

Preschool child _____
_____
_____
_____

School-age child _____
_____
_____
_____

Comparison _____
_____
_____
_____

3. Now interview the preschooler and the school-age child about friendship, using such questions as, "What does it mean to be a good friend?" "Why is it nice to have a friend?" "How can you tell that someone is a best friend?" Again, take notes on the children's responses. What stage of friendship understanding is each child at?

Preschool child _____
_____
_____

School-age child _____
_____
_____

Comparison _____
_____
_____

85

Applying Your Knowledge: Learning Activities (continued)

4. Identify a friend or acquaintance who is a member of a minority group, and ask permission to interview him or her about personal experiences in forging an ethnic identity. What challenges did this individual face, and how did he or she attempt to resolve them?

_____
_____
_____
_____
_____
_____
_____
_____
_____
_____
_____

CHAPTER 12

MORAL DEVELOPMENT

PARTICIPANTS

Katherine	18 months	Blue shirt, blue striped overalls
Braxton	15 months	White shirt, black pants
Alison	4 years	Blond hair, green dress
Stephen	4 1/2 years	Brown shirt with picture of deer, brown pants
Zacharie	4 years	White shirt with pictures of tractors
Liesl	7 years	Long dark hair, white and flowered shirt

- Preschoolers enrolled at the Child Care Center, Illinois State University
- Sixth through eighth graders, Thomas Metcalf Laboratory School, Illinois State University
- Six- and 7-year-old members of the Student Council (SRC), Swallowcliffe School, suburban Adelaide, South Australia

SUMMARY

The child's developing moral sense is depicted in this section, beginning with the emergence of compliance and cooperation in the second year of life. Emphasis is placed on the impact of child temperament and parenting strategies—in particular, firm, consistent discipline and a warm caregiver–child bond—on early moral internalization. Development of moral reasoning from middle childhood to adolescence is illustrated. On a distributive justice task, 7-year-old Liesl shows a strong commitment to sharing equally, no matter how much each child has contributed to a project. And when asked to respond to a story that taps prosocial reasoning, Liesl reveals her concern for maintaining friendships and helping others in need. A visit to a student council meeting at Swallowcliffe School highlights factors that support moral understanding, including peer interaction and opportunities for young people to participate in the governance of their community.

TAPE LOG
To view this section, cue tape to: 1:31:40.

MASTERING COURSE CONTENT

1. The narrator opens this section by stating that cognition, emotion, and social experience combine to influence the child's developing moral sense. After reading Chapter 12, provide an example of the influence of each factor on moral development.

Cognition _____

_____

Emotion _____

_____

Social behavior _____

_____

2. What cognitive capacities permit 18-month-old Katherine to comply with her parents' request to put away the toys? (506)

_____

_____

_____

3. Although Katherine can comply, she is also capable of saying "No!" For children who experience warm, sensitive caregiving and reasonable expectations for mature behavior, should toddlerhood be called "the terrible twos?" Why or why not? (506)

_____

_____

_____

_____

4. How is Katherine's newfound ability to follow adult directives likely to lead to a rise in parental expectations over the next year? (507–508)

_____

_____

_____

_____

5. Explain why Zacharie's temperament makes Joanna's efforts to socialize him more challenging? (483)

_____

_____

_____

_____

6. Which of the following parenting techniques would you recommend for Zacharie? (483)

   A. Mild, polite requests when he disobeys
   B. Firm, patient insistence that he comply
   C. Extra steps to build a warm, caring relationship
   D. A and C
   E. B and C

Explain your answer. _____
_____
_____
_____

7. Why is it important for Joanna to resist losing control when Braxton's anger is out of control? (483, 485)
_____
_____
_____
_____

8. What child behaviors probably led the child-care teacher in the Observation Program to place the two boys in time out? Why is time out useful as a disciplinary strategy under these conditions? (486)

A. _____
_____
B. _____
_____

9. Why are the distributive justice and prosocial dilemmas illustrated in the Observation Program more appropriate for young children than are Kohlberg's moral dilemmas? (501)
_____
_____
_____
_____
_____
_____

10. What is meant by distributive justice? Record 7-year-old Liesl's response to the distributive justice dilemma. At what level of distributive justice reasoning is she? (503–504)

A. _____

B. _____

C. _____
_____

11. Now record Liesl's response to the prosocial dilemma. At what level does she fall in Eisenberg's sequence of prosocial reasoning? Explain your answer. (504–505)

A. _____
_____
B. _____
C. _____
_____
_____

12. In student council meetings at Swallowcliffe School, children discuss and

participate in the formulation of school policies. Cite evidence on the role of such experiences in the development of moral understanding. (497)

_____
_____
_____
_____
_____
_____
_____
_____

13. How do the staff at Swallowcliffe School encourage children to solve social problems constructively rather than through aggressive, antisocial means?

_____
_____
_____
_____
_____
_____
_____

BUILDING CONNECTIONS

1. Recall from Chapter 9 (page 373) that toddlers typically display a vocabulary spurt between 18 months and 2 years of age. During this time, they also show rapid gains in self-control, as measured by delay of gratification (see Chapter 12, page 507). Is the acquisition of language related to the capacity for self-control? How would you explain this relationship? (Hint: Review Vygotsky's ideas on the role of language in development, Chapter 6, page 260–262.)

_____
_____
_____
_____
_____
_____
_____
_____

2. Research in the text indicates that moral reasoning is only moderately related to moral behavior (see Chapter 12, page 499–500). Besides cognition, emotion influences moral action. Describe emotional influences on morality, noting factors discussed in both Chapters 10 and 12.

_____
_____
_____
_____
_____

3. Look ahead to Chapter 14, and read the description of *authoritative parenting* on page 563–564. After reviewing research on the relationship of child-rearing practices to moral development (Chapter 12, page 497), explain why authoritative parenting is linked to moral maturity.

_____
_____
_____
_____
_____

4. According to many investigators of morality, out of experiences in dividing up resources fairly and deciding whether or not to act prosocially, Liesl *constructed* notions of distributive justice and prosocial obligations. Explain how this view is consistent with Piaget's *constructivist* approach to cognitive development (Chapter 6, page 222).

_____
_____
_____
_____
_____

Building Connections (continued)

5. Can the efforts of the staff at Swallowcliffe School to involve parents in their children's education and to provide children with networks of social support help combat the negative impact of poverty on development and improve children's school performance? Explain. (Chapter 14, page 562; Chapter 15, pages 635–636.)

A. _____

_____

_____

B. _____

_____

_____

_____

APPLYING YOUR KNOWLEDGE:
LEARNING ACTIVITIES

1. Visit a preschool or child-care center and watch for instances in which (a) children must divide up resources fairly, and (b) a child violates a moral rule—for example, by hitting or taking someone else's belongings. Record at least five such instances along with peer and adult reactions. Describe how these experiences provide children with opportunities to *construct* notions of fairness and justice.

A. _____
B. _____
C. _____
D. _____
E. _____

_____
_____
_____
_____
_____

2. Explore school-age children's understanding of distributive justice by presenting the following dilemma, illustrated in the Observation Program, to two children between 5 and 8 years of age:

> All these boys and girls are in the same class together. One day their teacher lets them spend the whole afternoon making paintings and crayon drawings. The teacher thought that these pictures were so good that the class could sell them at the fair. They sold the pictures to their parents, and together the class made a whole lot of money. Now all the children gathered the next day and tried to decide how to split up the money. What do you think they should do with it? Why? Should a child who made more paintings get more money than the others? Why? How about a child who doesn't have enough money to buy lunch everyday? How much money should he get? Why?[1]

Record the children's responses, and classify them according to the sequence on page 484 of the text. Do your findings match the text discussion of distributive justice reasoning?

Younger child: _____
_____

Older child: _____
_____

_____
_____
_____

_____

[1]Adapted from W. Damon (1977). *The social world of the child*, p. 66. San Francisco: Jossey-Bass.

Applying Your Knowledge: Learning Activities (continued)

3. Explore young children's prosocial understanding by presenting the following dilemma, illustrated in the Observation Program, to two children between 4 and 8 years of age:

> One day a girl named Mary was going to a friend's birthday party. On her way she saw a girl who had fallen down and hurt her leg. The girl asked Mary to go to her house and get her parents so the parents could come and take her to the doctor. But if Mary did run and get the child's parents, she would be late for the birthday party and miss the ice cream, cake, and all the games. What should Mary do? Why?[2]

Record the children's responses, and classify them according to the sequence on page 485 of the text. Do your findings match the text discussion of prosocial reasoning?

Younger child: _____

_____

Older child: _____

_____

_____

_____

_____

---

[2]From N. Eisenberg (1982). The development of reasoning regarding prosocial behavior. In N. Eisenberg (Ed.), *The development of prosocial behavior* (p. 231). New York: Academic Press.

CHAPTER 13

DEVELOPMENT OF SEX-RELATED DIFFERENCES AND GENDER ROLES

PARTICIPANTS

Emily	3 years	White blouse, pink and purple patterned jumper
Zacharie	4 years	White shirt with pictures of tractors
Alison	4 years	Blond hair, green dress
Stephen	4 1/2 years	Brown shirt with picture of deer, brown pants
Shawn	5 years	Blue striped shirt
Justin	6 years	Green shirt

• Preschoolers and kindergartners at Metcalf Laboratory School and at the Child-Care Center, Illinois State University
• Eighth graders at Metcalf Laboratory School, Illinois State University

SUMMARY

Gender typing—the process of developing gender-linked beliefs, roles, and self-perceptions—is the focus of this section. Toy choices and play activities of preschoolers reveal its beginnings in early childhood. Contributions of children's play styles and preferences to gender segregation are discussed, and emphasis is placed on the joint contribution of biological and environmental factors to gender typing. Sibling influences and adult encouragement of traditional gender-role behavior are explored, along with ways that teachers can reduce gender typing in preschool and elementary school classrooms. Development of gender constancy is illustrated by 5-year-old Shawn's and 6-year-old Justin's beliefs about whether changing a doll's clothing would result in a change in sex. The impact of puberty and perspective taking on gender-role identity in early adolescence is considered as eighth graders talk about their own and their peers' sex-related capacities and behaviors.

> ## TAPE LOG
> To view this section, cue tape to: 1:37:46.

MASTERING COURSE CONTENT

1. Gender stereotyped play and toy choices increase over preschool years. Explain how the rigidity of young children's gender typing is a joint product of cognitive immaturity and environmental influences. (524)

_____

_____

_____

2. The narrator, along with the text, points out that gender typing is especially strong for boys. Why is this so? (535, 536)

_____
_____
_____
_____

3. As the Observation Program illustrates, boys tend to play more actively and roughly than girls, who prefer quieter activities. According to research, what accounts for this consistent sex-related difference in play styles? (528–530)

_____
_____
_____
_____
_____

4. How do boys' and girls' play-style preferences join with environmental influences and cognitive factors to promote gender segregation? (528–529)

_____
_____
_____
_____
_____
_____
_____

5. Alison's mother commented off-camera that Alison rarely plays with dolls. Instead, she likes vehicles and construction toys. Alison has an older brother. What does research say about sibling influences on gender typing? (537)

_____
_____
_____
_____

6. According to the text and the Observation Program, what often happens in preschool and child-care settings that fosters compliance and dependency in girls and independence and self-reliance in boys? (549)

_____
_____
_____

7. What can teachers do to increase the chances that boys and girls experience a balanced array of activities—both adult-structured and unstructured. Provide two suggestions, one from the text and one from the Observation Program. (549)
A. _____
B. _____

8. Compared with preschoolers, school-age children have a more open-minded view of what males and females can do. What accounts for this change? (525)

_____
_____
_____

9. In one of the video segments, a sixth-grade boy in Spanish class accepts a purse

offered to him by the teacher. Then, after checking for the reaction of his classmates, he quickly removes the purse from his shoulder. Why did the boy become concerned about violating gender-role behavior in front of his peers? (536–537)

_____
_____
_____
_____
_____

10. True or False: According to cognitive-developmental theory, gender constancy is a major, organizing force behind gender-role behavior and gender-role identity. (540)

11. True or False: According to social learning theory, modeling and reinforcement promote gender-role behavior, and only then do children think about their actions and develop a gender-role identity. (539)

12. Record 5-year-old Shawn's and 6-year-old Justin's responses to the gender constancy task. Does the performance of these children fit with findings reported in the text? Explain your answer. (539)
A. _____
B. _____

_____
_____
_____
_____
_____

13. Cite biological, cognitive, and social influences on the rise in gender typing that typically occurs in early adolescence. (541)
Biological _____
Cognitive _____
Social _____

14. Note gender stereotypes revealed by the discussion among eighth graders in the Observation Program.

_____
_____
_____
_____
_____
_____

15. How does the eighth graders' discussion illustrate the finding that gender-stereotyped beliefs vary greatly from child to child. (526)

_____
_____
_____
_____

BUILDING CONNECTIONS

1. Select one of the following sex-related differences treated in earlier chapters: eating disorders in adolescence (Chapter 5, page 209–210); learned helplessness and achievement motivation (Chapter 11, page 455); or intimacy of friendships (Chapter 11, page 471). Explain how gender-role expectations contribute to the difference.

_____
_____
_____
_____
_____
_____
_____
_____
_____
_____

2. Look ahead to Chapter 15, and read the section on television and gender stereotyping on page 619–620. Cite examples of gender stereotypes children are likely to learn from TV. To what extent do you think television contributes to the view of many school-age children that although males and females *can* cross gender lines, males especially *should not* do so.

_____
_____
_____
_____
_____
_____
_____

3. Recall from Chapter 9 that girls show faster vocabulary growth in early childhood, after which boys catch up. But once in school, a sex-related difference in verbal ability reappears; girls are ahead of boys in reading and writing achievement. How might adult responsiveness to girls' early language advantage contribute to their school achievement in the verbal areas? What other influences—intrinsic to the child and in the social environment—do you think are involved?

_____
_____
_____
_____
_____
_____
_____
_____
_____

APPLYING YOUR KNOWLEDGE:
LEARNING ACTIVITIES

1. Many adults hold gender-stereotyped beliefs about what is appropriate for baby boys and baby girls. Interview the parents of a young infant. Find out whether they purchased certain colors of clothing or toys on the basis of the infant's sex. Ask the parents to describe their baby. If the baby is a boy, do the parents use more "masculine" descriptors, such as "active" and "loud?" If a girl, do they more often mention "feminine" characteristics, such as "gentle" and "sweet?" What expectations do the parents have for their child's behavior at older ages? Are they aware of gender stereotypes? Are they consciously trying to avoid them?

_____
_____
_____
_____
_____
_____
_____
_____
_____
_____
_____
_____
_____
_____
_____

2. Visit a child-care center or preschool and watch for instances of gender typing in children's behavior—for example, gender segregation and choice of activity environments. Next, note teacher behaviors that may encourage and sustain traditional gender-role behavior or, alternatively, promote gender-role flexibility. (For example, do teachers encourage children to play in a gender-typed fashion? Do they more often assign girls to structured activities, thereby promoting compliance and dependency?) Record your observations and compare them with research reported in Chapter 13.

_____
_____
_____
_____
_____
_____
_____
_____
_____
_____
_____
_____
_____
_____
_____

Applying Your Knowledge: Learning Activities (continued)

3. Watch television for a half-hour period at three different times of the day when young children are likely to view (early morning, late afternoon, and evening). List traditional gender-role themes and behaviors for a look at the extent to which TV conveys gender-stereotyped messages to children.

Viewing Period 1: Time of Day _____
Program: _____

_____
_____
_____
_____
_____
_____
_____
_____

Viewing Period 2: Time of Day _____
Program: _____

_____
_____
_____
_____
_____
_____
_____

Viewing Period 3: Time of Day _____
Program: _____

_____
_____
_____
_____
_____
_____
_____

CHAPTER 14

THE FAMILY

PARTICIPANTS

• Bill, a 24-year-old divorcé and custodial parent of two children: Dylan, age 5, and Jeremy, age 4, who has cerebral palsy
• Jane, age 38, and Emily, her 3-year-old daughter, adopted in the People's Republic of China
• Rachel, age 16, and her 89-year-old grandfather, Rabbi George Gordon
• Deb and Ron, age 36, a dual-earner married couple and parents of two children: Charles, age 4, and Maggie, age 1
• Karen Stephens, director, and children at the Child Care Center, Illinois State University

SUMMARY

In power and breadth of influence on children's development, no context equals the family. This section depicts the diversity of family lifestyles. Bill, a custodial parent of two sons, describes the pain of his divorce; why he took custody of Dylan and Jeremy; and his efforts to develop a career that will offer Jeremy, severely disabled with cerebral palsy, a secure future. Jane represents the increasing numbers of adults adopting children from foreign countries. Emily, her 3-year-old daughter, was born in the People's Republic of China and reared in an orphanage for the first 18 months of her life. Jane describes Emily's early development and her desire to help Emily merge her two cultural heritages: Chinese and American. Rachel, age 16, and her 89-year-old grandfather, Rabbi George Gordon, speak about what it has meant to live in the same city for the first time in each of their lives. Deb and Ron represent the dual earner marriage. The Observation Program depicts their busy schedule, the role of social supports in the workplace and extended family, and the challenges and rewards of combining career with parenthood. The ingredients of good child care are discussed by the director of Illinois State University's child care center.

TAPE LOG
To view this section, cue tape to: 1:42:19.

MASTERING COURSE CONTENT

1. According to the social systems perspective on family functioning, *third parties* can serve as supports for children's development, or they can undermine children's well-being. Who are the third parties that assist Bill, a single parent, in rearing Dylan and Jeremy? (560)

_____
_____
_____

2. Although more fathers are being granted custody after parental divorce, the arrangement is still unusual. Why did Bill take custody of Dylan and Jeremy?

_____

_____

_____

_____

3. As the text explains, parents affect children's development; children, in turn, profoundly affect parents' lives. How has parenthood—especially, caring for a severely disabled son—changed Bill?

_____

_____

_____

_____

4. How is paternal custody likely to benefit the development of Bill's sons? (580)

_____

_____

_____

_____

5. Jane, also a single parent, adopted her daughter Emily in the People's Republic of China. What special child-rearing challenges do adoptive parents face? (575–576)

_____

_____

_____

_____

_____

6. Emily, like many adopted children, had a stressful early life. She spent her first 18 months in unstimulating surroundings and was malnourished. Yet today she is doing well. What does research indicate about long-term developmental outcomes for adopted children? (576)

_____

_____

_____

_____

_____

7. Jane is taking steps to make sure that Emily merges her two cultural heritages—Chinese and American. At what period of development do adopted children start to become curious about their roots? Why is it important for Jane to enable Emily to have access to her culture of birth? (576)

A. _____

_____

B. _____

_____

8. How has living in the same city as her 89-year-old grandfather enriched Rachel's development? Do these consequences resemble those on extended-family influences,

reported in the text? Explain. (571)

_____
_____
_____
_____

9. What factors beyond the family make combining work and parenthood difficult for Deb and Ron? (585)

_____
_____
_____
_____
_____

10. What steps have Deb and Ron taken to ease work–family role conflict for Deb? How is Ron's participation in child rearing likely to affect their children's development? (584)

A. _____
_____

B. _____
_____
_____
_____
_____

11. The narrator comments, "To Joanna, Jane, and many other employed parents, high-quality child care is vital for protecting their children's development." Describe research findings on the developmental consequences of good-quality and poor-quality child care. (585–586)

_____
_____
_____
_____

12. The ingredients of good child care are discussed by the director of Illinois State University's Child Care Center. List factors she mentions, and compare them to the signs of high-quality child care for preschool children listed on page 586. Indicate, for each factor, whether the Child Care Center meets or exceeds the standards recommended in your text.

_____
_____
_____
_____

13. Why is it difficult for parents of young children to find good, affordable child care in the United States? (586–587)

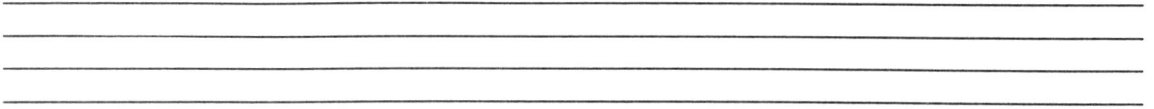

Name _____

BUILDING CONNECTIONS

1. Reread the description of resilient children on page 10 of Chapter 1. Off-camera, Jane mentioned to Professor Berk that the caretakers in the Chinese orphanage where Emily spent her first 18 months referred to Emily as "little smart" because of her outgoing, persistent personality. How might these personal characteristics have contributed to Emily's resiliency? In listening to Jane's description, what other factors did you note that probably helped Emily spring back from adversity?

A. _____
_____
_____
_____
_____

B. _____
_____
_____
_____
_____

2. Is living close to her grandfather likely to foster identity development in 16-year-old Rachel? Explain. (Chapter 11, pages 456–457)
_____
_____
_____
_____
_____
_____
_____

3. What impact is Deb and Ron's sharing of child-rearing responsibilities likely to have on Charles and Maggie? (Chapter 13, page 535, and Chapter 14, page 584)
_____
_____
_____
_____

APPLYING YOUR KNOWLEDGE: LEARNING ACTIVITIES

1. Rearing children successfully requires parents to extend their social networks. List individuals, organizations, and institutions with whom parents must interact to support their children's development during each of the following phases of development. Note how these supports for effective child rearing expand into middle childhood and then contract as children move closer to adulthood. Explain why this happens.

Infancy and toddlerhood (birth to 2 years): _____
_____
_____

Early childhood (2–6 years): _____
_____

Middle childhood (6–11 years): _____
_____

Adolescence (11 years on): _____
_____
_____
_____
_____
_____

2. For accreditation by the National Academy of Early Childhood Programs, the Child Care Center at Illinois State University meets rigorous standards of quality. Obtain a copy of those standards by contacting the National Academy of Early Childhood Programs, c/o the National Association for the Education of Young Children, 1509 16th Street, N.W., Washington, DC 20009-5786, telephone (800) 424-2460, www.naeyc.org. Select one of the following topics: physical setting, group size and caregiver–child ratio; daily activities; or teacher qualifications. Read the National Academy recommendations for preschool-age children, and justify them on the basis of your knowledge of child development research.

_____
_____
_____
_____
_____
_____
_____
_____
_____
_____
_____
_____
_____
_____

CHAPTER 15

PEERS, MEDIA, AND SCHOOLING

PARTICIPANTS

• Children at Thomas Metcalf Laboratory School, Illinois State University, preschool, elementary, and junior high classrooms
• Teachers and children at Swallowcliffe School, suburban South Australia, primary classrooms

SUMMARY

This section begins with an overview of the development of peer sociability, from isolated social acts in infancy to the complex social exchanges and group memberships of middle childhood and adolescence. Then the Observation Program visits several primary classrooms at Swallowcliffe School, which serves mostly poverty-stricken families. A new administration has transformed the school from a run-down neglected state into a unique, special place where cooperative learning takes place at all levels. Teachers team-teach in multigrade classrooms, guiding children in acquiring cooperative learning skills as early as age 5. Older children tutor and support younger children, and when peer difficulties arise, teachers and pupils come up with joint solutions through class meetings and other collaborative problem-solving techniques. Parent involvement in children's learning is central to the success of Swallowcliffe's educational program.

```
TAPE LOG
To view this section, cue tape to: 1:52:39.
```

MASTERING COURSE CONTENT

1. The narrator indicates that caregivers' affection and encouragement carry over to children's interactions with one another. Describe evidence presented in the text that parents influence peer sociability, peer acceptance, and peer group membership. (602, 605,607, 610–611, 614)
Peer sociability _____
_____
_____

Peer acceptance _____
_____
_____

Peer group membership _____
_____
_____
_____

2. Review the illustrations of how peer interaction changes from infancy to adolescence in the Observation Program. Then highlight major advances in peer sociability, based on research reported in your text. (599–601)

Infancy and toddlerhood _____

_____

The preschool years _____

_____

Middle childhood and adolescence _____

_____

_____

3. The narrator notes that peer groups become important contexts for social learning at adolescence. What do adolescents gain from peer group membership? (609–612)

_____

_____

_____

_____

_____

4. Multigrade grouping is central to Swallowcliffe School's educational philosophy. Cite positive outcomes associated with placement in multigrade classrooms (633–634).

_____

_____

_____

_____

_____

5. Swallowcliffe School makes a concerted effort to involve parents in their children's education. How can parent involvement foster children's learning? (635–636)

_____

_____

_____

_____

_____

_____

_____

_____

_____

6. Why might the cooperative learning approach at Swallowcliffe School be well suited to accommodating children with disabilities in regular classrooms? (635)

_____

_____

_____

BUILDING CONNECTIONS

1. In middle childhood, children's capacity to collaborate with peers improves (as the narrator notes) because of gains in social cognition. Return to Chapter 11, pages 463–467. Describe social-cognitive milestones that support peer collaboration.

_____
_____
_____
_____
_____
_____
_____

2. Cooperative learning can help ensure that children's classroom experiences are challenging and involve communication and collaboration. What characteristics make cooperative learning effective? (Chapter 6, page 265–266.)

_____
_____
_____
_____
_____
_____
_____
_____
_____

3. At Swallowcliffe School, teachers show children how to collaborate. What Vygotsky-based concepts are consistent with this approach? Explain. (Chapter 6, page 261.)

_____
_____
_____
_____
_____
_____
_____

4. At Swallowcliffe School, older children tutor and support younger children. What are the benefits of peer tutoring for both tutors and tutees? Explain how such benefits probably arise in the peer tutoring situation? Why is it important for adult teachers to train and supervise peer tutors? Do you think such training takes place at Swallowcliffe School? (613)

_____
_____
_____
_____
_____
_____
_____
_____

APPLYING YOUR KNOWLEDGE:
LEARNING ACTIVITIES

1. Arrange to observe for a 1- to 2-hour period in an elementary, junior high, or high school classroom. Indicate whether or not the following characteristics, which support academic and social learning, were present. For each characteristic, describe precisely what you saw.

Small class size _____
_____

Challenging learning activities _____
_____
_____
_____
_____
_____

Learning activities that involve communication and collaboration _____
_____
_____
_____
_____
_____

Teachers who promote high-level thinking _____
_____
_____
_____
_____
_____

Teachers who are responsive and encouraging _____
_____
_____
_____
_____
_____

ANSWERS TO

GETTING READY: REVIEW OF BASIC CONCEPTS AND THEORIES

BASIC ISSUES

1. A, C, B, F, D, E

2. A *stage* is a qualitative change in thinking, feeling, and behaving that characterizes a particular time period of development. Rapid development of representation, in terms of language and make-believe play, at the end of the second year, fits the definition of stage.

3. stability

4. True

Resilient Children

5. A. Personal characteristics of children: a calm, easy-going, sociable disposition; self-confidence; willingness to take initiative

    B. A warm parental relationship: a close, supportive relationship with at least one parent who provides affection and assistance and introduces order and organization into the child's life

    C. Social support outside the immediate family: a grandparent, teacher, or close friend who forms a relationship with the child

6. A. Reducing environmental risks; when many pile up, they are increasingly difficult to overcome

    B. Enhancing relationships at home, in school, and in the community that inoculate children against the negative effects of risk.

Contemporary Theories

Piaget's Cognitive-Developmental Theory

7. Children actively construct knowledge as they manipulate and explore their world.

8. C, D, A, B

9. A. Piaget's cognitive-developmental perspective has stimulated more research on children than any other single theory.

117

B. Piaget's theory convinced many child development specialists that children are active learners whose minds are inhabited by rich structures of knowledge.

C. Piaget's theory encouraged the development of educational philosophies and programs that emphasize discovery learning and direct contact with the environment.

10. A. Research indicates that Piaget underestimated the competencies of infants and preschoolers.

B. Evidence that children's performance on Piagetian problems can be improved with training raises questions about Piaget's assumption that discovery learning rather than adult teaching is the best way to foster development.

Information Processing

11. a symbol-manipulating system through which information flows.

12. To map the precise steps individuals use to solve problems and complete tasks

13. A. Like Piaget's theory, the information-processing approach regards children as active, sense-making beings who modify their own thinking in response to environmental demands.

B. Unlike Piaget, the information-processing approach does not assume that cognitive development takes place in stages. Rather, the view of development is one of continuous increase.

14. A great strength of the information-processing approach is its commitment to careful, rigorous research methods to investigate cognition.

15. A. Aspects of cognition that are not linear and logical, such as imagination and creativity, are all but ignored by information processing.

B. Information-processing research has largely been conducted in artificial laboratory situations.

Ethology

16. Ethology is concerned with the adaptive, or survival, value of behavior and its evolutionary history.

17. A. Imprinting is the early following behavior of certain baby birds that ensures that the young will stay close to the mother and be fed and protected from danger.

118

B. Imprinting led to the concept of the critical period.

18. A sensitive period is a time span that is optimal for certain capacities to emerge and in which the individual is especially responsive to environmental influences. Its boundaries are less well defined than those of a critical period.

19. John Bowlby's ethological view of attachment emphasizes the role of built-in social signals in encouraging the parent to approach, care for, and interact with the baby. The drive reduction explanation regards the baby's desire for closeness to the mother as a learned response based on feeding.

Ecological Systems Theory

20. Ecological systems theory views the child as developing within a complex system of relationships affected by multiple levels of the surrounding environment.

21. C, D, A, E, B

22. Important life events, such as the birth of a sibling, entering school, or parents' divorce, modify existing relationships between children and their environments. The timing of these changes affects their impact. Furthermore, as children get older, they select, modify, and create many of their own settings and experiences.

Vygotsky's Sociocultural Theory

23. Sociocultural theory focuses on how culture—the values, beliefs, customs, and skills of a social group—is transmitted to the next generation through cooperative dialogues between children and more knowledgeable members of society.

24. False

25. B

26. True

27. According to the dynamic systems perspective, the child's mind, body, and physical and social worlds form an integrated system that guides mastery of new skills. The system is dynamic, or constantly in motion. A change in any part of it—from brain maturation to physical and social surroundings—disrupts the current organism–environment relationship. Then the child actively reorganizes his or her behavior so the various components of the system work together again, but in a more complex and effective way.

28. Researchers are attracted to this new view because they want to do a better job of explaining the wide variation in development.

SUGGESTIONS FOR
OBSERVING AND INTERVIEWING YOUNG CHILDREN

Below are some suggestions for observing and interviewing young
children that will help you avoid common difficulties encountered by individuals new
to these experiences.

ASKING PERMISSION

Explain to the child's parent, guardian, or teacher what you want to do and why
you want to do it. Then ask permission to observe or interview. For children 3 years
and older, provide the child with an age-appropriate explanation and ask if he or she
would like to participate. For example, you might say to a young child, "I want to
know how children your age play these games and how they answer some questions.
Would you like to help me?"

Ask permission, even if you are observing in a public place. Parents (and some
children) are likely to become uncomfortable when they see you watching and do not
know the purpose of your activities.

OBSERVING

Observer Influence

Making observations always entails the risk of *observer influence*—the
possibility that due to your presence, children and adults will behave in unnatural
ways. To handle this problem, become acquainted with those you wish to observe,
and build an image of a friendly, nonevaluating individual by explaining what you
are doing to parents and teachers—and to children who are old enough to
understand.

Before beginning, spend some time in the setting so children become accustomed
to your presence. Most infants and preschoolers readily become used to being
observed; they cannot stop being themselves for very long. For older children, a
longer adaptation period may be necessary.

You can, to some extent, check whether your presence affected children's behavior.
After you have observed, ask the parent or teacher whether the child's activity
differed from what is typical.

Recording Observations

Review the procedures for observing on pages 44–45 of the text. If your goal is to
collect a broad range of information, use the *specimen record,* a description of
everything said and done over a certain time period. Jot down notes as you watch,
filling in missing information as soon as you have finished observing. Even better,
whisper a description of the child's activities into a tape recorder, and transcribe
your remarks as soon as possible. If you are interested in only one or a few
behaviors, *event sampling*—a description of all instances of a particular behavior
during a specified time period—is a more efficient procedure. Alternatively, you can
use *time sampling* by preparing a checklist of the behaviors of interest and

indicating whether each occurred during a series of brief time periods. For example, you might watch the child for 15 seconds and check off behaviors during the next 15 seconds, repeating this process until the observation period is complete.

INTERVIEWING

Rapport Building

So far as possible, sit so you are facing the child. Begin by establishing rapport; for example, ask the child about his or her interests and recent experiences. If the child is reluctant to talk, play a game that requires little or no verbal interaction, such as throwing and catching a ball. This gives the child a chance to feel comfortable with you.

Orienting Materials

Make sure you orient materials toward the child rather than yourself. A line of chips in conservation of number or a set of straws of different lengths in seriation looks quite different to a young child when viewed from the side rather than head-on. If you are not careful about orienting materials, you may not get responses that are representative of the child's thinking.

Phrasing Questions Clearly

Phrase your questions specifically enough to the child so there is little opportunity for ambiguity. For example, when giving conservation tasks, do not merely say, "Are these the same?" (too vague) Refer to the dimension of the task you have in mind: "Is there the same amount of (or just as much) water in both of these glasses, or does one glass have more water?"

Asking For Justifications

Many tasks that reveal children's thinking require that you ask for a justification of the child's answer. There are many ways to do so. Sometimes being asked "why" makes children uncertain of their response, since they may have come to associate the question "why" with being wrong. Rehearse several ways of asking for explanations, such as "What makes you think that?" "How come you think so?"

Avoiding Negative Feedback

When a response is incorrect, avoid saying so. Simply accept it as the child's view of the world. If you feel a need to give feedback, say something like this: "I see what you mean?" or "I see how you understand that."

From Berk, L. E. (1996). *Suggestions for observing and interviewing young children.* © Laura E. Berk, reprinted by permission.